The author and publishers of 'The Sixth Form MBA' are pleased to support MyBigCareer

MyBigCareer is a Charity which aims to break down the barriers to social mobility by helping underprivileged young people achieve their real potential through the medium of one-to-one careers guidance. Founded in September 2013, the importance of the Charity's work and aspirations has been recognised by politicians across all Parties, with Nick Clegg, the Deputy Prime Minister, Matthew Hancock, the Minister of State for Skills and Enterprise, and Meg Hillier, MP for Hackney South and Shoreditch, all having articulated their support. Dr Vincent Cable, the Business Secretary, is patron. London-based, the charity plans to expand across the UK so that as many young people as possible receive credible careers advice, regardless of background. A portion of the author's royalties will be donated to the charity.

To

Troy + Jillian

Good luck in your careers + happy reading!

D0907357

Critical acclaim for *The Sixth Form MBA* and Susan Croft:

"An indispensable guide to equip every reader with an insight into the world beyond formal education. This is a must-have for every sixth form school and college library."

Deborah Streatfield, Founder of MyBigCareer

"Equipping school leavers with skills that will help them to navigate the increasingly crowded job market is important for the future of work. Susan's new book fills a gap providing easily digested, useful advice for sixth formers about how to manage themselves in the job market and workplace. Her wide experience of the world of work and how to present yourself effectively to clients and potential employers shines through."

Kandy Woodfield, Director of Learning, NatCen Social Research

"This long-overdue book has many useful tips and advice for any Sixth Form student either going on to University or straight into full-time employment. The essential skills Susan Croft covers will prepare any 15-18 year old for life after school in a highly-competitive market... as someone who regularly uses the skills of interns and graduates, I can highly recommend this book. My own 17 year old is now enthusiastically reading her copy!"

Allyson Stewart-Allen, CEO, International Marketing Partners; Cranfield list of 100 Women to Watch

"For most people, the social and professional skills necessary for leadership don't come readily. That is why this book is so welcome. The best leaders are those who relate well to people, who are interested in others and are comfortable in social and professional surroundings. This book offers real insights into the principles of success and valuable advice on how to carry them into practice."

Sir Malcolm Grant, Chairman NHS Commission; former Provost UCL

"I thoroughly recommend this book as a concise, yet wide ranging introduction to some of the key soft and hard skills that students will need to acquire as they enter university. Understanding the rudiments of business and the associated competencies are life skills that outside of a formal postgraduate MBA course are not usually formally taught. This book provides students with just that - a quick guide to those skills that everyone talks about, but which are often learnt by default."

David Game MA (Oxon) MPhil (Lond) Principal of David Game College and Chairman of the David Game Group

"The Sixth Form MBA is simply a career bible you can refer to throughout your professional journey. The knowledge you get from this book will lay a solid platform for career development. Susan has presented invaluable content of knowledge in this book and it's really useful for any sixth former interested in the key skills for career development."

Duminda Pelmadulla, Group Financial Accountant, Unilever UK

"In the hectic world that Sixth Formers live in, they can often find that they take their eye off the ball of personal development. Yes exams are important, getting in to uni is important but so too is preparation for the world of work. This handy guide incorporates skills Sixth Formers need for the here and now (revision techniques, team-work skills, presentation skills) with those they will need in the soon-to-come, here-faster-than-you think future (negotiation, personal branding and networking). This book is a handy resource, not just for education but for the world of work."

Gareth Roberts, Assistant Principal and IB Co-ordinator, Hockerill Anglo-European College, Hertfordshire

"At last! Something that equips young people to deal successfully with the practicalities of life after schooling, rather than specialisms and subjects. How to get on is so much more important than how to get by. Susan has painted on a broad canvass; I wish I'd had this help when I was leaving school. Use this and, whilst there is no guarantee of success, at least you start ahead of the game."

Lord Digby Jones, Former Director-General of the CBI & Minister of State for Trade & Investment, and BBC TV's New Troubleshooter.

The Sixth Form MBA

Everything you need to know for career and personal success which is not covered in your school text books

Susan Croft

Thorogood Publishing Ltd
10-12 Rivington Street
London EC2A 3DU
Telephone: 020 7749 4748

Email: info@thorogoodpublishing.co.uk
Web: www.thorogoodpublishing.co.uk

A CIP catalogue record for this book is available
from the British Library.

ISBN:

Paperback (10) 1854188267 (13) 9781854188267

Ebook (10) 1854188674 (13) 978184188670

Printed and bound in Great Britain by
Marston Book Services Limited, Oxfordshire

For Alan

Table of Contents

The author

Susan Croft is the author of two previous books – *Win New Business* and *Managing Corporate Reputation* – both published by Thorogood. She lives in Brighton and Sarasota, Florida. This book is based on the workshops which she and her colleagues at CareerSkillsPlus deliver for schools across the UK. If you are interested in contacting her about workshops and summer schools, please email <u>scroft@asctraining.net</u>.

Follow us on Facebook and Twitter:

facebook.com/sixthformmba

twitter.com/SixthFormMBA

Introduction

By author Susan Croft

As the author of this book, I am very pleased you have chosen to read it and I hope you will find it a useful guide on the most important things you need to know to succeed in higher education (apart from passing exams and getting good grades – and this book can even help you do that, see Chapter 6 on memory skills) and the world of work.

You can start with any chapter you like, they are meant to be stand-alone guides, but I would suggest that you consider reading the book chronologically so that the case study is a little more meaningful.

There is little doubt that you are entering a world of strong competition, constant change and a high noise level in terms of the messages and signals you will be bombarded with. This book will help you navigate this world in terms of giving you advice on all the skills you will need to develop in order to succeed.

Before I review the chapters with you, let me introduce myself, and my fellow contributors.

I have taught career skills to thousands of sixth form students throughout the UK and USA. I am a co-founder of a company called Career Skills Plus and we run workshops, summer schools, enterprise days and sixth form inductions for schools and academies. I have written two previous books – both on business subjects – and I am delighted to have the support of my excellent contributors in bringing this book to you.

I am also a director of a company specialising in mobile learning – Skill Pill M-Learning – and we provide training refreshers and reminders to mobile devices in short, animated videos. We currently work with major businesses, and may one day bring our solutions to schools as well.

John Dalton, who wrote the chapter on memory skills, is currently Vice Principal and Head of Science at a leading independent college in London and has over 25 years' teaching experience in biology. He has taught memory and learning skills all over the UK as an independent consultant and has a particular interest in how students learn. He has been a witness for a *Guinness World Records* memory record and has helped many students improve their learning and memory skills. He has an extensive knowledge of how sixth forms function and has helped thousands of students enter university. John is also the director of a Medical and Life Sciences course and specialises in medical teaching. John graduated in biochemistry and is a Chartered Biologist who also takes students on ecology field trips for their A-level exams. Before becoming a senior teacher, he was managing editor of *Current Opinion in Gastroenterology,* one of the world's leading medical journals.

Dr Cristina Sambrook, our contributor on personal branding, is a senior consultant at Positive Presence, a London-based image consultancy. She has enjoyed a successful international career in both the private and public sectors as a consultant and project manager. Dr Sambrook has lived in several countries and worked in Romania, Israel and the UK on political campaigns, foreign investments and law.

Positive Presence is renowned internationally for having taken image consultancy to a respected and intelligent level through its Perception Management business. Working with men and women of all ages, Positive Presence Perception Management has successfully helped thousands of people gain credibility, gravitas and confidence, be viewed more positively, create meaningful relationships, and raise their profile.

Cristina also teaches at the University of Birmingham's business school. Her frequent interactions with young people made her realise the importance of building an executive presence as early as possible in one's career, and how enormously helpful this is in the process of getting a job. As you walk through the door, it is you who wins or loses the business, or gets the job or the promotion, through your personal impact and others' positive perceptions of you. Those crucial first impressions relate, of course, to appearance too. Looking groomed, well-presented and appropriately dressed has a big impact and will help increase the chances of forging that dream career.

Bruce Hoverd, author of the chapter on team working, is an experienced consultant and trainer and has taught a variety of business skills to sixth form students in the UK. He is a director of Career Skills Plus and during his distinguished career has worked for five very different organisations in five sectors. He is now a director of a change consultancy, working with a wide range of organisations, and runs his own company, Managing Pressure, which specialises in coaching individuals and supporting groups in dealing with stress and pressure, as well as building their resilience and influence. Programmes he delivers include Negotiating Skills, Dealing with Conflict, Managing Pressure and Developing Team Resilience.

He has recently worked with diverse organisations such as British Gas, Amey, Channel 4 and the European Central Bank. He works throughout Europe, the Middle East, Asia and Africa.

Angus Cater, our contributor on ethics and finance (not a tautology!), was first introduced to the world of personal finance at the age of 19 when he embarked on his formal training to be a stockbroker. Since then he has qualified as a financial adviser, both generically and for the leading advice firm St James' Place, trained as an accountant and completed an MA in finance. Angus has founded and run small businesses both in the UK and the US, and for the last 20 years he has run a financial business providing products to parents and students at independent schools. He is also director of Career Skills Plus.

In the early 2000s, when his children were embarking on university and new careers, and the financial ante of university education was beginning to rise, he was approached by the Girls' Day School Trust to help prepare their sixth form students for the tortuous process of managing their finances through university and beyond. Interviews with newly qualified students demonstrated how limited their financial knowledge was and the many mistakes which they had made and regretted. For the last ten years, Angus has given young people a practical framework for financial control whilst making it relevant and interesting. His chapter in this book attempts to distil those lessons onto the printed page. Today, young people can expect to invest upwards of £50,000 in their tertiary education and the financial choices they make will shape their whole lives. Angus hopes that his contribution to this book will assist them to make more good choices than bad ones.

Caroline Hopkins is founder of MindLab based in the UK. At the start of her career she set up HJ Associates, one of the first hospitality companies, in 1986, creating and producing hundreds of events for the boards of many household- name companies as well as after-show parties for rock stars. Time management and planning were key to making the experience as stress free and enjoyable for her clients and her project teams. She was also a governor of two schools and this experience, combined with her own daughters' time in the sixth form (now aged 22 and 20), served as a reminder of just how challenging the sixth form can be! Caroline is passionate about 'upskilling' with Mindfulness techniques, as she has seen at first hand that it not only prepares students for the sixth form but also for life.

Caroline encountered Mindfulness whilst recovering from a back problem, exacerbated by stress. Having benefited from the power of this, she realised that the science-based, non-religious Mindfulness training could be a very useful tool for everyone to embed in their lives if it could be taught in an accessible way. In 2010 she met Louise Chester, a global City analyst, who attributes her very successful career to Mindfulness. Together they set up Mindfulness at Work Ltd www.mindfulnessatwork.com in 2010 with the shared vision of taking Mindfulness in to the workplace and beyond so that hundreds of thousands of people could benefit. They developed the Mindfulness is Now (MIN) training course, which is taught for 45 minutes each week over four weeks.

Dr Gail Elaine Davies also works for MindLab. She has always had a passion for both science and education and has been fortunate to be able to combine both. She graduated from Oxford University with a degree in Biochemistry and remained there to pursue a Postgraduate Certificate of Education specialising in Biology. She secured a post as a Clinical Biochemist in a London teaching hospital and later followed her interest in human genetics by undertaking a PhD funded by the Medical

Research Council at St Mary's Hospital Medical School (Imperial College, University of London). She remained at Imperial College for 18 years, during which time she undertook a number of research projects, culminating with her own research which focused on Chromosome 21 and the genetics of Down's syndrome. In addition to securing grants, publishing papers and speaking at international conferences, she was involved in the Human Genome Project as a member of the Chromosome 21 consortium.

In 2002 Gail was part of the successful bid for London IDEAS Genetic Knowledge Park, one of the six centres of excellence funded by a government initiative. The remit was to provide a genetics information service for both health professionals and members of the public. During this time she designed and ran practical courses for students wishing to study genetics or medicine, chairing sixth form conferences to stimulate interest in biological sciences.

Gail started yoga in her first year at Oxford and this allowed her to find some peace and stillness in a sometimes quite stressful and hectic environment from the pressures of studies and career to those of coping with a family. Gail's interest in yoga grew and she pursued this by training to teach yoga and becoming an integrated yoga therapist using Mindfulness. She is currently undertaking a Masters in Mindfulness-Based Cognitive Therapy at Oxford University.

CASE STUDY

There is a case study running through the book which addresses the learning in each chapter. Here is an outline of the case study and the ways in which it relates to the content of the book:

Your school is gaining a reputation for academic excellence and is now launching a major campaign to recruit more pupils in all years. You have been asked to put together a team of fellow sixth formers – years 12 and 13 – to deliver the following programme:

• Position your sixth form against competitors in your geographic catchment area

• Build a reputation for academic and pastoral excellence

• Publicise sixth form achievements in local and national media

• Work with alumni to help raise the profile of your sixth form

• Recruit 10% more new students into the sixth form every year for the next two years

• Encourage students in years 10 and 11 to stay on to the sixth form rather than joining a competitive sixth form college or academy

• Leave a legacy programme that can be continued by other students once you have left school

CHAPTER ONE
Management and Leadership Skills

Chapter Overview

In this chapter we look at the nature of management and what it takes to be a good leader. We will consider the difference between management and leadership and help identify your strengths as a leader and the skills you need to be building. We will examine different management and leadership styles, and help you develop leadership skills for school, university, and the workplace.

So why should I care about developing management skills?

You may be fed up with hearing from parents, family members and your teachers how important it is to develop management and leadership skills. Indeed, you may also think that you are never going to be a manager, neither are you interested in business and, as for leadership, that's for those who want to run large companies or premier league football clubs.

In reality, having some good management skills will be very useful whether you become a teacher, scientist, veterinary surgeon, lawyer, artist, designer or, in fact, in any field of work. As for leadership, you may well have to lead a team at university; you may even now be taking on a leadership role in school. Certainly, when you move into the world of work, you will have many opportunities to demonstrate leadership skills, whether you choose to pursue them or not.

Question: Do you think there is a difference between management and leadership?

Let's take a look at the **function of management** as summarised by Sir John Harvey-Jones:

> *"Management, above everything else, is about people. It is about the accomplishment of ends and aims by the efforts of groups of people working together. The people and their individual hopes and skills are the greatest variable and the most important one."*

Essentially, management is about organising and planning so it helps if you are someone who can focus on a specific project, understand what needs to be done and by whom, and have the skills to monitor progress. Managers must also delegate tasks and allow people to take measured risks. They need the ability to motivate people, particularly through stressful times and when deadlines are looming.

- **Key point:** Occasionally the management and leadership roles overlap, so it helps if a manager also has some leadership qualities as well as the ability to inspire those who work for him.

These are the qualities of an effective manager:

- Well organised

- Attention to detail

- Good interpersonal skills

- Good communicator

- Directed in actions

- Good time management

There are generally four different management styles:

TELL – This style tends to be quite authoritative with very little input from those who are being told.

SELL - This style of manager seeks to 'sell in' her ideas and solutions, planning to win approval and agreement from those being managed.

CONSULT – The consultative management style is very participative. The manager actively seeks the views and ideas of others and takes them on board before making decisions

JOINT - This management style is the most participative. The manager provides his views and then delegates final decision-making power to the team members.

Question: Which style of management do you prefer?

Why do people stay in jobs?

Much has been written about this important subject and it is important for all organisations to understand how to retain people, particularly their top talent.

- **Key point:** Research shows that people stay in their jobs when they:

  - Have a manager who demonstrates interest and care

  - Have effective and appropriate feedback

- Know what is expected of them

- Have a role that fits their ability

"90% of employees leave managers, not companies."

Question: Which management skills do you possess? How have these been demonstrated at school, in summer jobs you have held, work placements, out-of-school activities? Are there any management skills you would like to develop?

Now let's take a look at the leadership function.

Leader's toolkit of qualities, attitudes and behaviours:

- Willingness to take risks

- Ability to suspend judgement

- Patience

- Respect

- Trust

- Honesty

- Curiosity

- Good listening skills

- Empathy

- Appreciation for diversity of thought, cultures, races, generations

- Open-mindedness

- Ability to give and receive constructive feedback

- Sees mistakes and failures as learning opportunities

- Transparency in management style

- Celebration of learning

- Shows appreciation and gives praise to others

Question: Which leadership skills do you possess? How have these been demonstrated at school, in summer jobs you have held, work placements, out-of-school activities? Are there any leadership skills you would like to develop?

Famous Leaders from History and Their Stories

LEADERSHIP LESSONS FROM QUEEN ELIZABETH I - A WOMAN IN A MAN'S WORLD

(Taken from Queen Elizabeth I by Alex Axelrod.)

Most people in Elizabethan England took it for granted that women were not only intellectually and temperamentally unsuited to leadership, but morally incapable of it as well. Male leadership was consistent with the rule of God and nature. Female leadership was not. When Elizabeth ascended to the throne her answer to these objections was a combination of prudence, boldness and genius.

She prudently surrounded herself with able advisers, chosen for their ability rather than out of personal affection. She also skilfully blended advisers from the past with those of her own choosing, thereby creating a sense of continuity accompanied by change rather than sudden, discordant revolution.

The boldness was rooted in Elizabeth's style of command. She used her formidable intellect, shaped by years of tutelage under some of the most able minds of her age, to make herself absolute mistress of the facts impacting on her realm: the political situation, the economic situation, the religious situation. She used her equally formidable ability to read human character – again, a faculty developed by necessity during the perilous years of her upbringing when every friend was a potential enemy – as a tool to penetrate and analyse the needs, desires, and intentions of those around her. Elizabeth issued decisive, even imperious commands. She took a 'buck stops here' approach to leadership, framed in bold statements and expressed through bold actions.

Finally came the genius. All effective leaders appreciate the power of image, and they strive to develop about themselves an image of leadership suited to the psychology of those they lead. Elizabeth thoroughly understood the culture from which she and her people sprung. As far as women were concerned, this culture favoured two convergent ideals: the glamorous law of chivalry and the courtly tradition of the feminine ideal – virginal, fair of hair, willowy and ethereal. Thus the queen portrayed herself – and allowed others to portray her – as an earthly incarnation of the Virgin.

LEADERSHIP LESSONS FROM MAHATMA GHANDI: THE POWER OF INTROVERTS

Gandhi was, according to his autobiography, a constitutionally quiet and shy man. As a child he was afraid of everything: thieves, ghosts, snakes, the dark, and especially other people. He buried himself in books and ran home from school as soon as it was over for fear of having to talk to anybody. Even as a young man, when he was elected to his first leadership position as a member of the Executive Committee of the Vegetarian Society, he attended every meeting but was too shy to speak.

"You talk to me quite alright," one of the members said to him, "but why is it you never open your lips to speak at a committee meeting? You are a drone." When a political struggle occurred on the committee, Gandhi had firm opinions but was too scared to voice them. He wrote his thoughts down and intended to read them aloud at a meeting. But in the end he was even too scared to do that.

Gandhi learned over time to manage his shyness but never really overcame it. He couldn't speak extemporaneously; he avoided making speeches whenever possible. Even in his later years he wrote, "I do not think I could or would be inclined to keep a meeting of friends engaged in talk."

But with his shyness came his unique brand of strength: a form of restraint best understood by examining little known corners of Gandhi's life story. As a young man, he decided to travel to England to study law, against the wishes of the leaders of his Modh Bania subcaste. Caste members were forbidden to eat meat, and the leaders believed that vegetarianism was impossible in England. But Gandhi had already vowed to his beloved mother to abstain from meat, so he saw no danger in the trip. He said as much to Sheth, the headman of the community.

"Will you disregard the orders of this caste?" demanded Sheth.

"I am really helpless," replied Gandhi. "I think the caste should not interfere in the matter."

If you read this story without a mention of Gandhi's name and later achievements, you might view the protagonist as a deeply passive man and, in the West, passivity is a transgression. To be "passive", according to the Merriam-Webster dictionary, means to be "acted upon by an external agency". It also means to be "submissive". Gandhi himself ultimately rejected the phrase "passive resistance", which he associated with weakness, preferring satryagraha, the term he coined to mean "firmness in pursuit of truth".

But as the word *satryagraha* implies, Gandhi's passivity was not weakness at all. It meant focusing on an ultimate goal and refusing to divert energy to unnecessary skirmishes along the way. Restraint, Gandhi believed, was one of his greatest assets.

"I have naturally formed the habit of restraining my thoughts. A thoughtless word hardly ever escaped my tongue or pen. Experience has taught me that silence is part of the spiritual discipline of a votive of truth. We find so many people impatient to talk. All this talking can hardly be said to be of any benefit to the world. It is so much waste of time. My shyness has been in reality my shield and buckler. It has allowed me to grow. It has helped me in my discernment of truth."

Question: Can you identify other leadership qualities that both Queen Elizabeth I and Ghandi possessed? Which other leaders do you think have also created a unique image based on the culture of their time?

Organisational Culture

One key area in any organisation which leaders influence is the culture of that organisation. Essentially, organisational culture is really about 'the way we do things around here'. Do staff members dress formally or informally? Does the organisation favour joint decision-making rather than more hierarchical management? Are people encouraged to try work stints in other departments or do they usually stay put in their own areas?

Take a look at the following types of organisational culture and think about which one appeals to you most. Culture can make a big difference when you are considering joining an

organisation and it can certainly affect whether you are happy there.

1. Power culture

Main characteristics:

- Depends on a central power source who influences the whole organisation and chooses like-minded people to get on with their jobs

- Organisation depends on trust and empathy

- Communication is telepathic or personal conversation

- Control is exercised by selection of key individuals, summonses to centre

- Proud and strong

- Reacts quickly

- Reliance on individuals

- Very competitive

- Judges by results and tolerant of means

- Usually small and focused on limited activities

2. Role culture

Main characteristics:

- Works by logic and rationality

- Operates well in stable environment

- Co-ordinated at top by narrow band of senior management

- The job description is more important then the person who fills it

- Personal power frowned upon

- Rules and procedures are major methods of influence

- Offers security and predictability for individuals

- Frustrating for individual who wants control over their work

3. Task culture

Main characteristics:

- Job or project-oriented

- Brings together the right people for the right job and lets them get on with it

- A team culture

- Adaptable

- Groups are formed for a specific purpose and then can be abandoned

- Thrives in a competitive market

- Expert knowledge is required

4. Person culture

Main characteristics:

- Individual at centre

- The structure only serves to support the individuals within it

- Influence is shared and the power is based on individual expertise

- Individual within it uses it as base upon which to build own career

Maslow's Hierarchy of Needs

As part of your school studies you might have come across the work of behavioural psychologist, Abraham Maslow, who believed that all human beings are motivated according to a hierarchy of needs as follows:

1. **PHYSIOLOGICAL** (Basic)

- Hunger

- Thirst

- Sleep

2. **SAFETY** (Emotional and physical)

- Security

- Protection from danger

- Shelter

- Absence of fear

3. **SOCIAL** (Group affinity)

- Belonging to groups

- Social activities

- Love

- Friendship

4. **SELF-ESTEEM** (Ego)

- Self-respect

- Status

- Recognition

5. **SELF-REALISATION** (Fulfilment/maturity/wisdom)

- Growth

- Personal development

- Accomplishment

The needs hierarchy is based on needs, not wants. It operates on an ascending scale – as one need becomes fulfilled the next is uncovered. People can revert back – someone operating at level four, for example, will revert to level two if a strong feeling of insecurity takes over. Once this need is satisfied, he or she will return to their former needs area. Needs which aren't being met are demonstrated in behaviour. Managers and leaders must create a motivational workplace environment and to avoid staff apathy, which often results when needs are unfulfilled, managers must be able to implement the right action at the right time.

Question: At which point in Maslow's hierarchy do you think a manager or leader plays a role?

In light of that question and your answers to it, let's take a look at the chart below:

Applying Maslow to business	
Maslow's hierarchy	**Business examples**
Step 5 - Self-actualisation	Opportunities for creativity and personal growth, promotion
Step 4 - Esteem needs	Fancy job title, recognition of achievements
Step 3 - Social needs	Good team atmosphere, friendly supervision
Step 2 - Safety needs	Safe working conditions, job security
Step 1 - Physiological needs	Salary, decent working environment

Motivation

This brings us onto the question of what motivates people – an important consideration for both managers and leaders.

If you are to maintain the motivation of individuals, you need to know what they expect to get out of their work. What kind of rewards are they seeking?

- Good wages or salary

- Prospects for promotion

- New challenges and change, opportunities to be creative

- Few challenges or changes

- Doing high-quality work

- High profile, personal status, power

- Personal and professional development opportunities

- Contributing to a worthwhile enterprise or cause

- Agreeable working conditions

- Freedom to control own work

- Lots of direction

- Social contact

- Convenience

If you don't know, you need to find out! The best way is to ask.

There are several general rules for motivating staff:

- Thank them for their efforts

- Praise them for work that is well done

- Criticise them constructively and only in the context of their performance

- Learn from your own mistakes and admit to them

- Be a partner – don't always take the credit for successes

- Show your commitment to the person and recognise theirs

- Include people in planning and decisions

- Communicate clearly and openly

Finally, there are many ways to destroy motivation:

- Keep staff in the dark about the real purpose of their work

- Make sure that you get the credit while they get the blame

- Never admit you might be wrong

- Give them work for which they are unsuited

- Let them get really involved in a serious mistake before intervening

- If they come to you for help, don't listen; respond with platitudes or false reassurance

- Harp on details while ignoring the real issues

- Don't give advance information about changes

- Discourage new ideas

- Insist that they do their job your way

- Make it clear that it never pays to step out of line

Let's now turn our attention to the important subject of ethics.

Angus Cater, one of this books contributors, has the following to say:

Why Do Ethics Matter?

It was Socrates who said: "The unexamined life is not worth living." What did he mean?

Ethical behaviour is particularly important if you are managing or leading people. History is littered with examples of wicked and unethical leaders as well as many examples of leaders who demonstrated tremendous personal integrity, goodness and right-mindedness in all their leadership actions.

We all know people who go through life acting without any regard for other people. Very few of us can claim to be perfect in our thoughts or behaviour towards others, but to fail to consider them at all makes a particularly unattractive human being.

In recent years, society has attempted to regulate our behaviour more, partly out of political idealism and partly out of despair at man's wickedness to his fellow man. So we now have rules (laws) which make it punishable to be racist or sexist and the concept of the 'hate' crime has become established in the lexicon, if not yet in a practical legal sense.

A variety of rules have sprung up to try and regulate the behaviour of those who work in financial services so that it is difficult to make money out of the gullible and financially naïve. None of this should be necessary; there have always been people who display the full range of a human's worst behaviour but they were always outnumbered by the mass of law-abiding, thoughtful, decent people. Did it all start in the eighties with the so-called greed of the Thatcher years exemplified in *Bonfire of the Vanities*? I am not sure, but I do know that it is impossible to regulate all the behaviour of human beings and that one should encourage self-regulation wherever possible. Which brings us to the important subject of ethics.

Ethics are about us and how we view the world. Our ethics, be they financial, sexual, or relating to some other aspect of our behaviour, shape us as a person and shape the way others see us. We therefore need to look hard at ourselves and think about what matters to us. Perhaps the key is the old saying: 'Do as you would be done by'. Would you want someone to steal from you, take advantage of your ignorance, exploit your need to survive by working you very hard for very little, lie about you, sell you something which didn't work properly, poison you, abuse your children and so on. One assumes not, and you might think this is all pretty obvious and guilt is our way of keeping us on the straight and narrow. But what happens when our ethical base is tested in a difficult live situation? For example, the day before your final exams at university, a friend tells you that he has had access to one of the papers. You have been alternating between a 2.1 and a First for your whole time at university and a really good result in this paper could secure you that coveted First. No one is going to get hurt – a victimless crime you might think. Well, not quite, because you are the victim. If that final exam does not properly test your knowledge, you will never know whether you got that First because you had worked for it and deserved it or because you were able to prepare the answers the night before. Nobody else gets to suffer except you. Your parents and friends will be overjoyed for you but you will know that you are a fraud and the consequences of that knowledge could be extensive. It could undermine your whole life's endeavour.

Another obvious example is the sports drugs cheat. What is the point of winning a gold medal if you know that it was not fairly won in a straight competition against your fellow athletes? Who is the loser here?

So, although there are ethical norms that we all mostly buy into (the Ten Commandments for instance), we have to create our own ethical framework against which we can test the dilemmas that come up every day in our lives. When we say that a person has no moral compass, we mean that he has no ethical framework and is blown hither and thither by every breeze that wafts through his or her life. Don't let that be applied to you.

Putting Your Action Plan Together: Developing Leadership Skills

You need to make sure that you are strong in the basic management skills before you can become an effective leader. Are you confident in your ability to communicate, delegate, build teams, handle difficult situations, deal with all kinds of people and make decisions?

If you feel ready to move on and develop leadership talent, here are some steps to take in order to do so:

- Identify three specific leadership strengths you have now

- Identify three specific leadership skills you want to work on

- Find at least two leaders to model your behaviour on – role models can be very helpful to you in all stages of your life

- Determine what these leaders do that constitutes effective leadership – try to get at least two specific ideas from each of them

- Establish your leadership development goals for the next month, year, three years

CASE STUDY

We will now turn our attention to the case study described in the introduction to this book. If you have not read it, please refer to the introduction.

As the project manager of this important campaign you will need to do the following:

• Select your team members and allocate roles

• Produce a strategic plan identifying objectives, stakeholders, budget and timetable of activities, and measurement benchmarks

- Establish lines of communication and reporting with your school's senior management team

- Ensure that your plan and strategy is in line with the campaign strategy for the rest of the school. Remember, your focus is the sixth form and you need to ensure that your plan is part of the larger school campaign

You will also need to be accountable for your actions, ensure that your team is motivated and properly directed (see Chapter 5 for more information on working in teams).

Before moving on to the next chapter, consider how you are going to tackle the above case study points.

Final Word

Those who make the best managers are people who have a well-developed, realistic sense of their strengths and limitations. You cannot be all things to all people. You cannot be perfect and you cannot achieve everything. It really does not matter how many books you read or courses you attend, effective managerial practice starts with your ability to manage yourself. This involves taking a critical and honest look at your actions and reactions to people and events and at the way you manage time and tasks in the workplace.

It means recognising the situations that you manage less than well and creating constructive ways forward for dealing with these, using your strengths. **There is no right style of management.** There is **your** style of management, based on a considered assessment of your capabilities and what you do well, as well as a clear identification of those areas that need development.

You will learn by experience and it's OK to make mistakes. Use your experience, with its mistakes as well as its successes, as learning opportunities. Take the time to reflect on and critically appraise your actions and reactions.

Chapter Summary

In this chapter we have looked at the differences between management and leadership and the key functions of both. We have also considered various styles of management and leadership and leadership hierarchy. We have also identified two very different leaders from history who made a huge impact on their countries. We have discussed different organisational cultures as well as Maslow's hierarchy of needs as it relates to management. We have looked at the important management and leadership function of motivating others, and finally, we have considered the subject of ethics and how important it is in both management and leadership.

We now turn our attention to one of the most important leadership skills – the ability to communicate effectively.

Further Reading

The Organisation of the Future, The Drucker Foundation (Jossey-Bass)

Elizabeth I CEO, Alan Axelrod (Prentice Hall)

The 7 Habits of Highly Effective People, Stephen Covey (Simon & Schuster)

Corporate Cultures, Deal and Kennedy (Addison Wesley)

The Six Pillars of Self-Esteem, Nathaniel Branden (Bantam Books)

What Colour Is Your Parachute? Richard Bolles (Ten Speed Press)

From Good to Great, Jim Collins (Random House Business)

Quiet: The Power of Introverts, Susan Cain (Penguin)

Principle Centred Leadership, Stephen Covey (Simon & Schuster)

Feel the Fear and Do It Anyway, Susan Jeffers (Arrow Books)

Mintzberg on Management, Henry Mintzberg (Free Press)

CHAPTER TWO
Influencing, Communication and Presentation Skills

Chapter Overview

We now turn to the important subject of communication and influencing. Getting your voice heard and making memorable and effective presentations is a critical skill at university and in the workplace. In this chapter we will look at ways to communicate with brevity and impact and will introduce you to different communication styles and behaviours. You will learn how to adapt your own style depending on different people and situations and use 'mirroring' techniques to gain positive outcomes in your communication encounters.

The Four Social and Communication Styles and How to Influence Them

How successful you are in your relationships with others (whether in the workplace, at school or socially) can be greatly affected by how you relate to each other and work together. A project is more likely to succeed when there is good 'chemistry' between the people involved. One way of assuring this is to select people who probably will or have worked well in the past together and are a good fit for the team.

Since this is often not possible, it is helpful to develop an awareness of interpersonal style and how it can be used to enhance personal effectiveness.

Starting with noted psychologist, Carl Jung, behaviourists have observed and categorised behaviour. This has led to the development of social and management style models that cluster certain behaviours around four styles. The model sets forth predictable patterns of behaviour and can be used to better understand one's own behaviour and that of others. This understanding can minimise friction when dealing with others and enhance understanding and co-operation.

Most social and managerial style models use a four-quadrant grid to interrelate two key dimensions of behaviour:

1. **Power or assertiveness** - the degree to which an individual asserts herself, controls and presents herself and her ideas with confidence, strength and assurance.

2. **Emotion or responsiveness** – the degree to which an individual reveals herself, emotions, feelings and impressions. In other words, how 'open' the person is.

The cross-referencing of these two dimensions produces four combinations of behaviours, each with its own typical behaviour and communication characteristics:

High assertion/high emotion = Expressive style

High assertion/low emotion = Controlling style

Low assertion/high emotion = Amiable style

Low assertion/low emotion = Analysing style

Let's look at each style, how they communicate and the hot button for each:

- **EXPRESSIVE** – also known as an activist style, this person likes to see the big picture and eschews minute detail. They enjoy working in an open-plan office environment, making it easier to interact with colleagues. This individual is often a multitasker and gets easily distracted. They frequently have quite messy work areas with lots of projects on the go. The key to influencing the expressive personality is to understand their hot button: **Get recognition and reward!** This individual will often have photos of themselves receiving an award or holding the cricket trophy!

- **CONTROLLING** – also known as the driver, this person wants to be captain of the ship. And if they are not yet in that position, they will be charting a course to achieve it as quickly as possible. This style is very goal-oriented and results driven. No giddy behaviour around this person. Their hot button is: **Get it done!** Expect to see certificates of achievement and congratulatory letters in their office.

- **AMIABLE** – the quintessential consensus seeker, this individual is an excellent team player. Their amiable personality will want to make sure everyone is on the same page. They are not happy with change so if you have to deliver news about change, best to tell them first what will remain the same. Your key to influencing this personality type is to understand their need for harmony in the workplace. Hot button: **Let's get along with one another!** Their office area may well have family photos on display.

- **ANALYSING** – thoughtful and somewhat circumspect, this individual is keen on accuracy. Don't expect snap decisions from your analytical personality – they like to mull things over. Send them agendas in advance, make sure you structure your meetings carefully and timetable everything. The analytical's hot button and the key to influencing them is: **Make sure you get it right!** Expect to see planning charts and certificates of achievement in this person's office.

Like most models developed with extensive research over time, it is generally valid. Obviously, some individuals will exhibit more extreme or rigid examples of a particular style than others. Also, people may adjust their behaviour slightly depending on their mood, their interest or the particular situation. But, by and large, people will tend to behave in a certain way and will exhibit the characteristics of their style.

The key to enhancing interpersonal effectiveness is **adaptability**. By understanding one's own style and those of others around us, we can begin to modify our behaviour to make the other person more comfortable with us. This is not manipulative, it is simply recognising the differences in the people we deal with and adjusting our behaviour appropriately in order to gain positive outcomes and good working relationships with others.

The Four Dimensions of Personality Type

The Type System of personality assessment, as developed by Isabel Briggs Myers and Katherine Briggs, is based on four basic aspects of human personality:

- How we interact with the world and where we direct our energy

- The kind of information we naturally notice

- How we make decisions

- Whether we prefer to live in a more structured way or in a more spontaneous way

These aspects of personality are known as dimensions because each one can be pictured as a continuum between opposite extremes.

Communication, particularly in the workplace, can be far more effective if one understands the dimensions of personality type.

How we interact with the world and where we focus our energy:

(E) Extraversion_____l_____**Introversion (I)**

The kind of information we naturally notice:

(S) Sensing_____l_____**Intuition (N)**

How we make decisions:

(T) Thinking_____l_____**Feeling (F)**

Whether we prefer structure or spontaneity:

(J) Judging_____l_____**Perceiving (P)**

The various combinations of the above dimensions result in 16 separate personality types.

The 16 Personality Types

Tick the following statements that apply to you:

Extrovert:

- Like being centre of attention
- Tend to think out loud

- Talk more than listen

- Energised by being with other people

- Communicate with enthusiasm

- Respond quickly – enjoy fast pace

- Prefer breadth to depth

Introvert:

- Avoid being centre of attention

- Think, then act

- Private people – share personal info with select few

- Listen more than talk

- Are energised by spending time alone

- Prefer depth to breadth

Sensors:

- Trust what is certain and concrete

- Like new ideas only if they have practical application

- Value realism and common sense

- Tend to be specific and literal

- Are oriented to the present

Intuitives:

- Trust inspiration

- Like new ideas for their own sake

- Value imagination and innovation

- Tend to be general – use metaphors, analogies

- Present information through leaps, in a roundabout manner

- Are oriented to the future

Thinkers:

- Value logic and fairness

- Naturally see flaws and tend to be critical

- Consider it more important to be truthful than tactful

- Believe feelings are valid only if they are logical

- Are motivated by desire for achievement

Feelers:

- Value empathy and harmony

- Naturally like to please; show appreciation easily

- Tactful as well as truthful

- Believe any feeling is valid, whether it makes sense or not

- Are motivated by desire to be appreciated

Judgers:

- Are happiest after decisions have been made

- Have a 'work ethic'

- Set goals and work towards achieving them

- Derive satisfaction from finishing projects

- See time as a finite resource and take deadlines seriously

Perceivers:

- Are happiest leaving options open

- Have a 'play ethic'

- Change goals as new information becomes available

- Derive satisfaction from starting projects

- See time as a renewable resource and deadlines as elastic

Relating To Others

In order to have successful working relationships with tutors, fellow students, bosses, colleagues, and the wider world it is important to relate well to others and see the world from their viewpoints. Here are some tips (identified by Dale Carnegie in his seminal book 'How to Win Friends and Influence People') to help you engage well with others and achieve positive outcomes in your college and working life:

1. Avoid over-criticising, condemning or complaining.

2. Recognise other people's efforts.

3. Be interested in other people's viewpoints.

4. Smile often.

5. Use a person's name to engage attention and build rapport.

6. Be a good listener. Encourage others to talk about their views.

7. Talk in terms of other people's interests.

8. Make the other person feel important and interesting.

9. Focus on points of agreement when trying to win an argument.

10. Show respect for the other person's opinions.

11. If you are wrong, conceding the fact will gain you respect.

12. Be sympathetic with the other person's ideas and desires.

13. Start by creating a friendly atmosphere.

14. Do not humiliate people over mistakes they have made.

15. Invite questions and feedback when giving orders.

16. Appreciate the efforts others are making. Praise is important.

17. Create an atmosphere that brings out the best in others. Help them aspire to their goals.

18. Use encouragement. Make any errors seem easy to correct.

19. Never use your authority to force someone to do something they don't want to do.

20. Never dismiss someone because of perceived prejudices. Remember you can learn something from just about everyone you meet.

Getting Your Voice Heard

We live in a society with a high noise level where, on a daily basis, thousands of messages are competing for our attention. Just think of your typical day in terms of what you see and hear: road signs, billboard advertising, text messages, e-mails, tweets, 24-hour news feeds on television and the internet, plus all the information and messages you receive at school through teachers, friends, films and other media. Bombarded with so much data, it's no wonder we have become selective listeners.

All this means that it is exceptionally important to be able to craft clear, succinct and compelling messages when you want to get your voice heard. This may be in a tutorial, seminar, lecture, meeting, interview or presentation. The ability to speak with authority and impact is a wonderful skill which will serve you well throughout your life. Let's look at some ways to do this:

- **Get to the point in your communication.** Determine what you want to say and convey your message succinctly and powerfully. There are generally two styles of communication: **inductive** and **deductive**. The inductive communicator likes to give a lot of background, context and detail before making a point. As an example, if you ask a truly inductive communicator 'What time is it?' you are likely to be told how a watch is made! Deductive communicators get to the point quickly. It's the style of communication used by the press and media. When you look at a newspaper, what do you read first? The headlines probably. Deductive communication is headline driven. So asking your deductive communicator "What time is it?" you will be told the time directly. Deductive communication is the opposite from rambling – try to be deductive when you want to convey an important message.

- **Avoid apologising before you speak.** If you want to be heard in a university seminar or at a meeting, do avoid apologies before you make your point. For example: "Sorry to interrupt" or "Maybe this isn't a great point, but...." or "I probably haven't really thought this through, but...." or, worse still, "This is probably not a good idea, but...." If you speak in this way, people will lose respect for you and will quite likely tune out on what you are subsequently saying. Be bold with your communication – have the courage of your convictions.

- **Remember to lean in when you want to convey a powerful message.** We also call this 'energy forward in your seat'. Instead of leaning back in your chair when you are speaking, position yourself in the forward half of it, keep your back and shoulders straight and maintain good eye contact with the other person. This helps you deliver your point with energy and enthusiasm as opposed to more of a laid-back, uninterested approach.

- **Listen attentively when others are speaking.** Listening is probably one of the most underrated communication skills. When you truly listen to others, it is essentially a gift you are giving. In our fast-paced, soundbite-driven world, we often forget to listen to others. We are so busy being distracted or thinking about what we are going to say, that we miss much of what we are hearing. **Some people truly listen – others wait to speak.** Which are you? Good listening means that you put aside your own thoughts as far as possible in order to focus on what the other person is saying. It also means that your body language and facial expression indicate to the speaker that you are listening to what they are saying. For example, direct eye contact, the occasional nodding or raised eyebrows, taking notes if appropriate, leaning in. Your response should also firmly indicate that you have heard the other person by adding to what they have said, clarifying a point they have made, paraphrasing their words, or asking a relevant question.

- **Use a strong tone of voice.** The way you speak can either detract from your message or strongly support it. Avoid speaking in a monotonous or timid way. Project your voice so others can hear you. Your voice should mirror your message. Take a look at the following study conducted by a team of social scientists at the University of California Los Angeles (UCLA) about what inspires trust and credibility in a communication. The study, led by Dr Albert Mehrabian, found the following breakdown in how messages are received:

Verbal (the actual words you speak) = 7%

Vocal (your tone of voice, cadence, intonation) = 38%

Visual (body language, non-verbal signals) = 55%

This is not to say that you can speak total rubbish in a strong tone of voice using positive body language. Verbal is of course critically important. But what the study reveals is that if your words are incongruent with your tone of voice and your body language, it is likely that people won't believe what you are saying and will not give you much authority and respect in the communication.

Making Effective Presentations

You will undoubtedly have to make many presentations whilst at university and you will certainly be called upon to present your ideas and proposals at work. Being able to make effective presentations and deliver impactful speeches is a key ingredient for success in the wider world. Let's look at some key tips to help you.

- Know your audience and craft your message/s to their needs and interests.

- Engage your audience using humour, anecdotes, examples, your personality (see below for three steps in engaging others).

- Plan your presentation and rehearse.

- Do not over-rely on power point slides and if you use them do not read every word on the slide – rather, paraphrase each slide and add additional information.

- Encourage questions. In your preparation you should anticipate likely questions and come up with good answers. Make sure you include tough questions as well as those you welcome. If you have a non-responsive audience, you can always ask a question yourself. For example, "When I gave this presentation last week, somebody asked me..."

- Remember your body language. Make it positive. The larger the audience, the more expressive and larger your gestures. See below for some guidance on speaking with body language.

How to engage your audience in three easy steps

1. KNOW THEM

Years ago I went to hear a well-known speaker talk to high school students at a local school. The students were informed and excited about the possibility of listening to this expert. It didn't take the speaker ten minutes to lose his audience. I remember whispering to my colleague, "Who does he think he's talking to? The board of trustees?" The students began whispering and the teachers tried to control the noise: some kids got up to go to the bathroom while others fell asleep. The speaker had a captive audience but no one was listening. Obviously, the speaker didn't spend any time getting to know his audience.

Be clear about your objective for the presentation. Do you want your audience to 'know' something, 'do' something, or a combination? The audience wants to know why they are there and what is expected of them.

Before you put pen to paper, make sure you know something about your audience. Ask yourself, what's the most important thing for me to know about them? Will my audience be decision-makers, the curious or prisoners being forced to be there? How much do they know about the topic? Are they 'big picture' or 'detail' oriented? Do they have concerns? What do they 'need' versus what do they 'want'? (How does their need fit into your objective of 'know' vs 'do'?) How might they react to the presentation? What are some questions or objections that might come up?

2. ACKNOWLEDGE THEM

Many years ago, I was participating in a conference and the speaker was a nationally known expert. Before she started her talk, she went up to every participant, looked them in the eye, shook their hand and said something. There were at least 75 people in the room! She took her time and connected with all of us. I don't remember what she said but I remember how I felt... acknowledged and connected.

Since then, I acknowledge the participants in my room before I start a presentation. I look them in the eye, maybe shake their hand, but I always say something to each of them before I start. And then, when I begin, I thank them all for being there. I acknowledge that they had other choices with their time and I appreciate them choosing this program.

I don't have any metrics to chart the effectiveness of this approach. I just know that my audience is engaged quicker and we seem to smile more.

3. LOOK AT THEM

What do we assume, in our culture, if someone doesn't look at us when they are speaking to us? Not interested? Not confident? Doesn't know the material? Eye contact is key in engaging your audience. Look at one person at a time, give them a piece of information (a sentence, a thought), PAUSE, find another set of eyes and continue the conversation. This approach works if you are speaking to a small group or to a large auditorium filled with people. This is a win-win skill. You will feel connected and they will feel engaged. Result!

Speaking with body language: the five parts of your body your audience is listening to

When you speak in public, you speak with more than your mouth. Effective public speaking isn't only about what you're saying, but how you say it. Public speaking anxiety can leave you looking nervous, afraid, and unprepared. Strong, confident body language is essential for a successful presentation. In the same way that users of American Sign Language portray complex thoughts and ideas with their bodies, your body language is telling your audience a story.

Here are the parts of your body to keep in mind while speaking in public:

Back, shoulders and neck

Do you remember your parents or teachers always telling you to sit up straight? Maybe they told you to stop slouching or told you to stop staring at your feet.

So take their advice. Take command of the room and your audience will pay attention. Neck, shoulders and back all play a role in making sure you maintain an assertive stance for your viewers.

Hands

How you use your hands will vary with the type of speech. Nervous fidgeting is a no-no. If you're giving a more serious, professional presentation, a confident grasp on the lectern will do. For more high energy presentations, use your hands to convey ideas. If you're discussing raising anything, a short gesture upwards will do. Hands can also identify board points or audience members with questions.

But don't overdo it! High energy is good, but crazy, frantic, or too fast and you may lose your audience.

Eyes

They say the eyes are the window to the soul. Do you want people to see someone scared and anxious, or do you want them to see a persuasive, inspiring leader? Nervous blinking, frantic gazing, and wide-eyed fear are common symptoms of public speaking anxiety.

Use your eyes to convey tone and emotion. A raised eyebrow or a cleverly timed wink can amplify a point.

Also use your eyes to identify with the audience. Great speakers can make eye contact with every viewer in the room. If the audience feels acknowledged, they'll be more open to your words and ideas.

Feet

Be aware of and control any nervous foot-tapping that may be disruptive during your speech.

If you're commanding a stage or a room, be sure to use those feet to move! You want to interact with your entire audience, not just those front and centre.

Mouth

It's more than just where your words come from. Don't let your fear of public speaking lead to lip-biting, lip-licking, teeth-grinding, tongue-clicking, and other mouth-related speaking flaws.

If you're keeping track of what your body is doing, you'll be sure to keep the attention of your audience and make an inspiring impact.

Communicating and Influencing by E-mail

E-mail is the least effective way to influence and needs to be balanced wherever possible with face-to-face, telephone and video conference contact.

First contact sets the tone so begin with a greeting and something which acknowledges the person, what they have been doing or what they have written to you.

Send only in a positive or neutral emotional state as anger or other negative emotions are transferred in the way you write, the language you use, !!!!!!, and highlighting. Taking time to reflect will allow you to write in a more unemotional way.

Be concise as others will stay attentive, get the key information and pick up specific messages.

Retain a structure to ensure that the receiver can follow your thinking process and ensure what you say will make sense.

Always do an 'If I was reading this' check or, even better, get someone else to read it first if it is really important. What will establish rapport? Use similar language and terminology.

Use plain and precise language that is free of jargon, suitable for the receiver and says exactly what you want. The use of signposting words helps to trigger others' attention, e.g. "I recommend...the two best options are...the main benefit will be..."

Use "I need" as "I want" seems strong language in written form, unless it is a positive request, e.g. for help. Also be explicit about what you need.

Stick to agreements on replying, actions etc. as other people will trust you more and will do less reading between the lines.

Use e-mail for mainly task or procedure activity where information, proposals, reasoning and facts are needed. Do not use for highly emotional issues.

Make limited use of 'cc' 'copy' and 'reply all' to show you think carefully, value others' time and are selective.

Check out your assumptions when you are replying, so that you confirm your reading and understanding to match what the others intended, e.g. "It sounds like you want me to...your main proposal seems to be that we..."

E-mail can be used as an avoidance tactic! If you need to say something important that requires you get a sense of how the person is really responding, then choose face-to-face or phone communication.

Tell the truth as it is important that others can believe what you say and trust you. In reply, be open if something does not make sense or if you have real concerns. Ask for clarification, further information or examples.

CASE STUDY

Well, our team has been busy allocating roles and responsibilities and creating a campaign plan identifying achievable goals and a programme of action. Your school's senior management team together with the board of governors has now asked you to meet with them to present your ideas and discuss the budget. You have invited two others in your team to present with you. You now need to do the following:

• Create a compelling, well-structured presentation outlining the key stages in your campaign.

• Determine who in your team will deliver which parts of the presentation.

• Rehearse with your team. Time each part of the presentation to ensure it fits the time allocated.

• Develop a campaign budget and ensure you have thoroughly checked all your anticipated costs. See the chapter on managing money for further information on this important area.

• Develop a list of questions you are likely to be asked and, together with your whole team (not just those presenting), come up with some sound answers.

• Have a final dress rehearsal to correct any problems and boost confidence. You might also invite the rest of the team to act as your audience and ask questions at the end.

Chapter Summary

In this chapter we have looked at various aspects of influencing others. In particular, the importance of understanding what makes others tick, and the ability to slightly shift your own style in order to get positive outcomes in all your working relationships. We have looked at the four dimensions of personality type and considered ways to successfully relate to others. We have also looked at the keys to effective communication, recognising that this is an essential part of good leadership. Finally, we have considered how to make memorable presentations and looked at the importance of engaging your audience and using positive body language. In the following chapter, we will consider an area of education and work which is becoming increasingly important: how to network and build lasting contacts for your future.

Further Reading

How to Win Friends and Influence People, Dale Carnegie (Vermilion)

Do What You Are – Discover the Perfect Career for You Through the Secrets of Personality Type, Paul Tieger and Barbara Barron-Tieger (Sphere)

How to Talk to Anyone, Anytime, Anywhere, Larry King (Crown Publications)

You Are the Message, Roger Ailes (Doubleday)

A Women's Guide to the Language of Success – Communicating with Confidence and Power, Phyllis Mindell (NYIF/ Prentice Hall)

Silent Messages, Albert Mehrabian (Wadsworth)

THE SIXTH-FORM MBA

CHAPTER THREE
Networking Skills

Chapter Overview

This chapter covers the techniques of working a room with ease and grace. You will learn the benefits of effective networking and how to make positive impressions when meeting people in a social environment. Good networking skills will serve you well at university and are very important in the workplace.

What is Networking?

Simply stated, networks are people talking to each other, sharing ideas, information, and resources. Networking is done in many ways, through conferences, professional associations, committees, phone calls, e-mails, air and train travel, lectures, workshops, parties, grapevines, mutual friends, meetings, newsletters and, of course, through social media.

Sociologists used to estimate that each of us knew about 250 people. This was our primary network. Today, many of us have access to thousands of people through school, university, work, friends, family and neighbours. Your base of contacts today is far larger than it ever could have been a decade or so ago and can include people on the other side of the world. Your common interests, contacts, information, support, referrals and recommendations can be shared just as readily over the web as in a meeting hall.

Effective networking is a very useful skill that will serve you in both your personal life and in your career. In many ways, networking is a lifestyle and needs to be incorporated into everything you do. It also needs to be appropriate to the occasion. This means that in varying social, education and work situations you are going to network differently. For example, networking at a business event is one thing, while networking at a school reunion is somewhat different, in that you will be playing a different role.

Networking is part of the process of developing your **social capital.** Building your social capital hinges on the development of meaningful relationships with other people. Since one should always be working on building meaningful relationships with other people, this probably means you should always be networking. However, that doesn't mean you should always be trying to 'sell' something to someone or be interested in meeting only those people who can help you. This approach rarely facilitates the development of meaningful relationships and gives networking a bad name. Some people think that networking means to be constantly selling yourself and what you do, but really effective networkers are more interested in giving to others and building valued and supportive relationships. It is important to keep your networking goals in sight at all events and opportunities, without becoming a networking vulture or someone that everyone else runs from when they see you coming. **Tailor your networking strategies so that you fit in without being tuned out.**

The beauty of networking is that it is not necessarily a gift you are born with. It is one you can learn and, the more you practise, the closer you are to becoming a successful networker. True, some people are naturally adept at making connections, but having been born with the personality of a television talk-show host is not a requirement for networking success! Nor do you have to have a computer-like brain to store all the names of people you've been introduced to.

Here are the key characteristics that make a successful networker:

- Commitment

- More interested in giving than getting

- Good listening skills

- Ready to follow up

- Able to ask for help or advice

- Be comfortable with sharing achievements

- Knowledge seeker

- Good memory

- Patient

- Good time management

Determining Your Networking Profile: Self-Assessment Exercise

Score yourself on a scale of 1 – 4 in terms of how much you agree with each statement and how it applies to you.

1 = Not at all

2= Somewhat/maybe

3= Most of the time/quite probably

4= Absolutely

1. I know the values and principles that are important in my life:

2. I can list five major achievements of which I am proud:

3. I know my strengths and how I can help others:

4. I introduce myself in a clear, concise and personable way that generates interest:

5. I am at ease in groups and can generate conversation in most situations:

6. I reintroduce myself to people rather than waiting for them to remember me:

7. I focus on people as they are introduced so that I can remember them:

8. I think I could be comfortable being the host at a networking event:

9. I am comfortable sharing my achievements and aspirations with others:

10. I have a daily action list and try to complete this each day with items transferred or crossed off:

11. I do what is in front of me rather than creating more items on my action list

12. I return phone calls, text messages and e-mails promptly:

13. I say no to events, activities, and meetings that drain my time, energy and focus:

14. I ask for, and use, the support of others:

15. I find opportunities to ask "Who do you know who...?"

16. I am an active and perceptive listener:

17. I approach each contact and opportunity with an open mind:

18. I am planning to join a professional group or club:

19. I would like to start a club or association:

20. I see the world as one big networking opportunity:

Scores:

60-80: You are a powerful and confident networker

40-60: You display good networking skills

30-40: You have some skills and need to work on others

Below 30: You tend to be rather shy and this will impact networking opportunities. Use the tips in this chapter to help you improve your skills

(Exercise adapted from Power Networking by Donna Fisher and Sandy Vilas)

Creating Networks

Now, whilst you are still at school, is the time to start building your networks; in fact, the greatest one is your own sixth form. Your school probably has an alumni association and, as soon as you leave, you will be invited to join. In this way you can keep in touch with teachers, the school and also the friends you made there. Some schools invite sixth formers to join the association even before they have left. If yours is one of them, do make sure to attend at least one alumni event before you leave.

You might also consider the following:

- Join a club related to your interests and career aspirations

- Be an active member of the club

- Start your own professional group or club

- Later on in life, when you are at university and at work, you should have your own business card. This should have your name, e-mail address, and mobile phone number. You might also like to develop an attractive logo for your card. Cards are invaluable tools in networking.

- Collect cards from others and develop a filing system for them. Effective networkers often create a database of contacts with basic information (name, phone, e-mail, etc.) plus other information such as birthday, interests, and where they met the person in question. Consider investing in contact database software or a personal digital assistant to help organise your contacts and manage your network.

- Follow up on those contacts you think you would like to stay in touch with. An e-mail or text message is fine.

- Consider finding a 'mentor' in your network – someone who can be a sounding board for career advice and other matters. This may be someone who is a role model for you, a person doing what you would like to do in life and who is open and willing to guide you. Often such mentors can become lifelong friends and counsellors.

- Develop your public speaking skills.

- Consider ways to use social media to increase your networks. In addition to Facebook, LinkedIn is a very useful resource and is used by professionals and business people all over the world.

- Read a daily newspaper and keep up with the news online. This will help broaden your horizons and facilitate interesting conversations at networking events.

Question: Which of the above appeals to you? Which ones will you start working on now? Consider other ways to develop your personal networks.

"*Making a good, positive first and last impression.*"

This is discussed in detail in Chapter 9 of this book, but meanwhile what do you think are the best ways to make good impressions on others?

Social Networking – Or How to Work a Room

Working a room is a risk and can be very intimidating. The idea of walking into an enormous ballroom with hundreds of strangers, all of whom seem to know one another, can fill even the most stalwart of us with fear and anxiety. Attending a party with strangers is one of the biggest social fears along with public speaking, according to a study on social anxiety reported some years ago in the *New York Times*. But if you approach the social event with confidence and a positive attitude, you can reap great rewards in terms of making friends and contacts, learning something new and just having a good time.

Networking can be tremendously rewarding, on both a personal and a professional level, and is a requirement nowadays in most jobs. In fact, many organisations require their staff to write brief reports after networking events covering who they met and what they learned. University, higher education, work experience and gap years will provide enormous networking opportunities. Do take advantage of them!

The benefits of being able to work a room with ease and grace are manifold:

- You can make invaluable business contacts, as well as starting new friendships that may last your whole life.

- It can be an ideal opportunity to cement relationships with others or correct misconceptions and problems that may have arisen in the relationship. It is often easier to do this in a social situation.

- It often provides a wonderful opportunity to gain new knowledge about your profession and interests in life.

- It can frequently help you with your career and career choices (never be afraid to ask for advice!)

- You feel better about yourself, motivated and ready to tackle anything.

- You make others feel more comfortable, which makes them want to be friends with you – an invaluable commodity in most jobs where 'chemistry' counts.

- You can become a powerful ambassador for your own organisation, often opening doors to promotion and career growth.

Let's now consider what the best networkers and socialisers have in common.

Question: Do you know someone who is a role model for you? Perhaps you can see him or her completely at ease at Number 10 Downing Street, or the White House, or attending a school reunion. They exude quiet confidence and are engaging to others. What does that person do that makes him/her so special and effective?

Here are some of my thoughts:

- They treat everyone as interesting and special. Isn't it true that the people we find most interesting and personable are those who seem most interested in us?

- They make others feel secure, and part of the occasion.

- They introduce people to each other; they remember names and something about those they introduce. In other words, they shift from 'guest' to 'host' behaviour. A good way to think about this is to consider a small orchestra. You are the conductor (the host) and you bring in the violins when required, then percussion and finally piano. A good conductor ensures that everyone in the orchestra plays when it is their turn and a good host makes sure everyone is included in the conversation.

- They have charisma; they smile; they draw others out.

- They are at ease with themselves; their charm is contagious.

- They are not vain or self-centred; they build self-esteem in others.

- They look at things from different angles.

- They have broad horizons.

- They are enthusiastic.

- They are curious and ask lots of questions, but their questions are non-invasive.

- They empathise with others.

- They have a sense of humour and are able to laugh at themselves.

- They have their own special style.

- They recognise different communication styles and use 'mirroring' techniques. Remember we discussed this in Chapter 2.

- They are generous of spirit.

Key point

Be generous of spirit. This was mentioned earlier in the chapter as it relates to master networkers. People who have high self-esteem and are comfortable with themselves always wish others the best. They are genuinely happy when someone they know gets a promotion or marries the perfect person. It's those without an ounce of self-esteem who hide in their rooms sticking pins in a voodoo doll or grinding their teeth when they hear of other people's good luck. Being happy for others elevates the spirit and demonstrates class and confidence.

Let's now imagine that you have been invited to a school alumni networking reception which will be held at a museum in your local city. Over 150 people are expected to attend representing different professions, jobs, universities and age groups. You will be attending with two other

people from your sixth form and have been asked to deliver a brief presentation about the event to the whole school the following day. You have also been asked to discuss the campaign you are working on for your school – i.e. the one that runs through this book as a case study.

Preparing for the Event

As with most important activities in life, preparation is important. Following are some things to consider in advance of the event:

- What are your objectives for attending?

- Research the venue. There should be a lot of information available about the museum on the web as well as in printed matter.

- If possible, obtain a guest list. Get background information on those you would like to meet – Who's Who, professional journals, Internet, personal biographies, etc.

- Research key people, guest speakers and any VIPs attending.

- Sort out logistics: what time do you want to arrive, how will you get there and home again?

- Broaden your horizons: be current with world affairs, read the news. Be prepared to talk about your own interests, particularly as they pertain to the event. Make a list of at least three things you can talk about – a play or film you've recently seen, a book you've read, something unusual in the newspaper that day.

- Consider what to wear: dress appropriately in order to blend in, rather than stand out! Keep flashy jewellery to a minimum. Wear comfortable shoes as you will be doing a lot of standing. Always ensure good personal grooming – check hair, nails, scuffed shoes, stains on clothing, etc.

- Jackets or suits say 'successful'. Avoid adjusting yourself (clothes, hair) while speaking. It diminishes your personal power. Stick with solid, dark colours in year- round fabrics. For the women, be careful with make-up, but by all means do wear some.

- Prepare your 'small talk' – weather, transportation, as well as the networking event itself are always safe topics. Identify areas of interest in your school or in the news which you can talk about with enthusiasm and knowledge. Think about the following subject areas: sport, films, books, public life, people and events in the news, as well as the latest news from your school. Make this part of your networking 'toolkit'.

- Plan your self-introduction –'the ten-second soundbite'. The ten-second soundbite is a brief, succinct and snappy description of who you are and/or the particular role you are playing at the event. Try to introduce yourself in a way that sparks interest, and remember to smile as you do so.

At the Event

OK, so we've prepared ourselves for this important event and how we want to make it fun and worthwhile, rather than trial by fire!

Enter the building and the networking room with confidence. Remember good deportment says a lot about you – keep your shoulders back, have a straight back, smile and look pleased to be there. We call this using the 'right entry language'. The speed and confidence of your gait should display awareness and a 'pleased to be here' attitude. Don't stand meekly in the entrance, but walk with deliberation into the room. Approach either a person standing alone or a group of more than two people.

- **Graceful entrances - how to join a small group of people you have never met before**

This aspect of networking fills most of us with trepidation and the fear of rejection. My advice is to abandon your fears and approach people with confidence and pleasure. They are fellow travellers like you and this is an opportunity to make new friends and contacts. A good way to break into a group is to approach groups of three or more people first, and stand on the periphery of the group within earshot and within eye contact of at least one member. When there is a pause in the conversation, introduce yourself, perhaps by adding a remark to the conversation. You might also be invited to join the group within a few seconds of standing there. So don't be shy – work the room!

If you are in a group and inviting someone else to join, do remember to recap the conversation for them: "Do join us. We were just discussing the guest speaker..."

In our society, we generally shake hands when we meet new people. In some countries they bow or kiss cheeks. A word or two about handshakes: make sure you have a strong one – nobody likes a limp handshake and people are often judged by the way they shake hands. Make sure you grip the whole hand from base of thumb to base of thumb. Look the person in the eye for as long as it takes you to identify the colour of their irises.

Graceful exits – how to move on at the end of a conversation

As with breaking into a group, exiting one, especially if it is just you and one other person, can also be quite challenging. You should be watching for signs from the other person that it is time to draw the conversation to a close. Such indicators might include distractive body movements, looking over your shoulder, more pauses in the conversation, etc. Following are some things you can say to draw things to a close, but do make sure that your exit is polite and that you thank the person and say how much you enjoyed meeting them.

- Say you need to make a phone call

- The host has asked you to circulate

- Introduce the person to a third party and, once they are in conversation, politely move on

- Offer to get the drinks

- Exchange cards with the individual and wish them a pleasant evening

- Mention that there are a couple of other people you would like to meet and that you need to circulate

Remember that first impressions count and so do **last** impressions, so make sure your exits are always graceful.

- Forgotten name? Ask for the person's business card, or ask him or her to write down their phone number

- If you have forgotten someone's name when making introductions (a nightmare for most of us), try to make them introduce themselves or use the connection gambit: "You two must meet since you are both keen mountain climbers!"

- Total panic – comment on room, organisation, furniture, paintings, event, speakers, weather. Always have a fall back

- Never criticise anyone to a stranger (especially the host!)

Drawing people out – copy royalty approach:

- How do you know the host?

- What is your connection with the organisation?

- Tell me about yourself

- Avoid the familiar, unless taking short rests on the circuit. Use this time to make notes on those you have met and want to contact later, as well as people you still wish to meet.

- Handling food and drink: it might be wise to take a short break from the social circuit to have a bite to eat, especially if the food is a little messy. It is difficult to speak, shake hands, listen, exchange cards, hold a drink and eat food all at the same time! Remember to check for stains once in a while. It is very embarrassing to come home from a party, look in the bathroom mirror and find spaghetti sauce on your blouse!

- Conversation techniques:
  - Opening a subject from cold
  - Adding to someone's else's comment

- – Bridging to the subject you wish to introduce

- • Using the bridging technique. Remember ABCD =

  - – **A**ddress the issue

  - – **B**ridge to your agenda by using a link phrase such as "that reminds me of" or "furthermore, let me say..."

  - – **C**ommunicate your **C**oncern

  - – Add a **D**angle or a new piece of interesting information

- • Remember that in most situations, conversation should be like a tennis game – back and forth with all participants serving new topics or adding fresh ideas from time to time.

Four steps in making the communication connection

1. Get the person's attention – show interest by asking questions

2. Add further interest by responding and eliciting more information, but don't move conversation on to yourself. This is known as 'autobiographical listening and responding'

3. Involve yourself in the other person's message by adding to what they say or asking further questions

4. Network by connecting one person to another or to resources you can provide

Ten ways to be a complete bore at a networking function!

1. Hijack the conversation

2. Brag about your achievements and focus solely on yourself

3. Interrogate others

4. Insist on one-upmanship

5. Constantly seek free advice or service

6. Interrupt others or finish their sentences for them

7. Refuse to share any information about yourself or your interests

8. Insist that your opinion is the right one

9. Come across as a bigot

10. Keep telling people they're wrong

Networking at seated functions:

Know who will be your table guests. If you are the host, try to arrange round tables rather than square or oblong. Introduce yourself to everyone. Make sure that each person is included at some point in the conversation. Involve the shy guest. Involve everyone with positive body language and direct eye contact. Remember when making introductions to introduce the most senior person first.

Finally, and very importantly:

Eight networking questions

These will help you in any situation, particularly in those not-so-golden silences, or when speaking to VIPs, or when you are in unfamiliar territory:

1. How did you start in your particular profession?

2. What do you enjoy most about your work?

3. What advice would you give someone just starting in your profession?

4. What one thing would you do in life if you knew you could not fail?

5. What significant changes have you seen take place in your profession through the years?

6. What do you see as the coming trends in your profession/business?

7. What's the strangest or funniest incident you've experienced in your business?

8. May I contact you again if I have any questions about the.................profession/business?

And always remember to thank the person in question. Never underestimate the value of a simple 'thank you'.

After the Event

- Effective follow-up is important and should be done within the next three to five days.

- Sort through the business cards you have collected – make notes on the back as a memory jogger later.

- Did you achieve your objectives? Was it worth your time and effort? Would you go again?

- Did you learn anything? How can you share this learning with others?

- Remember to send a thank you letter or e-mail to the host. This simple and gracious act is often overlooked and is something that will endear you to others and probably get you invited back.

MOST FREQUENTLY ASKED QUESTIONS AND ISSUES ABOUT HOW TO WORK A ROOM

Q: How can I overcome my fear of making a fool of myself or appearing like an outsider?

A: Prepare for the event: guest list, venue, logistics, knowledge bank, your self-introduction, be clear on the reasons why you are attending and whom you wish to meet.

Q: I worry that everyone will be looking at me as I enter the room and that makes me very self-conscious.

A: People will only look at you if you are dressed in a highly unusual way, if you are announced, or if you are very famous! However you should still enter the room with confidence, using positive body language.

Q: What's the best way to introduce myself to a group of strangers?

A: Approach groups of three or more people first, and stand on the periphery of the group within earshot and within eye con-tact of at least one member. When there is a pause in the con-versation, introduce yourself, perhaps by adding to the conver-sation.

Q: I'm always forgetting people's names. Are there any techniques to help with this?

A: You are not alone! Most people have difficulty remembering names and it gets worse as we get older! Here are two techniques which will help short-term recall. When you are introduced to someone, try to repeat their name out loud as soon as you can in the conversation. Alternatively, repeat the name quietly in your head and try to associate it with something or somebody. Word association can be a powerful tool.

Q: I'm always getting stuck with just one person at a social function and find it very difficult to extricate myself – any tips?

A: Yes, remember your graceful exit. Thank the person and say how nice it was to meet – wish them a pleasant time and move gracefully away. You might introduce the person to a third party or say that the host has asked you to circulate. The exchange of business cards is often a cue to move on. Never just walk away from the person leaving them high and dry in mid-sentence!

Final Word

Keys to Becoming a Master Networker

- Embrace the 'givers gain' philosophy

- Work your networks in a disciplined structure

- Plan your networking

- Find a role model or mentor

- Become a great storyteller

- Have a database of resources to help others

- Be open to new people and new ideas

- Make building relationships a part of your life

- Watch personal grooming

- Practice firm handshake and two to three-second eye contact when introduced

- Move from 'guest' to 'host' behaviour

- Remember your graceful entrances and exits

- Use bridging technique in conversation – it will help you drive the agenda and convey your key messages

- Keep one hand free to accept business cards and shake hands

- Take a break from the social circuit once in a while to enjoy the buffet and have a drink. It is very difficult to shake hands, exchange cards, hold a plate and a glass at the same time

- Remember to follow up as needed and send a thank you letter to the host if appropriate

CASE STUDY

Our campaign is going well, but we do need to get the views of the school's alumni and existing students. We therefore decide to put together a special reception to which we have invited 50 alumni of different age groups as well as students in years 11, 12 and 13 and the entire school staff. This is going to require our best networking skills as well as the ability to work well as a team.

Use the tips and techniques in this chapter to plan and deliver a wonderful networking event and turn yourself into the 'host with the most!'

Chapter Summary

In this chapter we have discussed the benefits of networking and considered the key traits of highly effective networkers. We have looked at ways to build networks and the importance of making good first and final impressions. We have considered three important aspects of networking – preparation, working the room at an event and follow-up. Finally, we have reviewed the keys to becoming a master networker. Now it is time to move on to something a little different, but equally important – **negotiation**.

Further Reading

The First Five Minutes: How to Make a Great First Impression in Any Business Situation, Mary Mitchell (Wiley)

You've Only Got 3 Seconds: How to Make the Right Impression in Your Business and Social Life, Camille Lavington (Doubleday)

Dig Your Well Before You're Thirsty: The Only Networking Book You'll Ever Need, Harvey Mackay (Doubleday)

How to Work a Room, Susan Roane (Harper Collins)

How to Gain the Professional Edge: Achieve the Personal and Professional Image You Want, Susan Morem (Checkmark Books)

Do What You Are: Discover the Perfect Career Choice Through Personality Type, Paul Tieger and Barbara Barron-Tieger (Sphere)

Masters of Networking, Ivan Misner and Don Morgan (Bard Press)

Win New Business – The Desktop Guide, Susan Croft (Thorogood)

CHAPTER FOUR
Negotiation Skills

Chapter Overview

In this chapter we will cover what is meant by negotiation and the key steps in a negotiation, particularly the importance of preparation and clear communication. We will examine the key traits of master negotiators as well as the pitfalls that many of us fall into when negotiating. Having good negotiation skills will prepare you well for both university and the workplace, where negotiation is a key skill.

Let's start by defining what we mean by negotiation. The word derives from the Latin *negotiari* – to do business. Here is the Oxford English Dictionary definition: "Negotiation is conferring with another with a view to compromise or agreement."

Here is another definition: "Negotiation is to work or talk with others in order to achieve a transaction, settlement or agreement."

Negotiation is the process through which two or more people (also referred to as parties) seek to achieve an agreement in their mutual interest, or for their mutual benefit. Negotiating is not necessarily a battlefield or a fight; it is an opportunity for everyone to get a result which they have positively contributed to and will act upon.

We negotiate regularly in our daily lives. This might be deciding with a friend which film you will both see, or where you might go for a weekend camping trip. Consider this simple question: are you a negotiator? The odds are that you thought "no" or "not really".

Consider another question: do you live with others, work with others, socialise, or have friends, parents, or siblings? Now ask yourself: do you ever have to make decisions or agreements with them?

The answer is almost certain to be "yes" and yet, in our domestic lives, we tend to ignore 'negotiation' as being part of what we do on a daily basis.

Most of us are born with innate communication skills, so we can let others know which of our basic human needs they should meet and when. We begin to use these communication skills, in a form of subconscious negotiation, from the moment we are born seeking warmth, comfort, food, attention and safety.

A newborn infant, waking its parents at two o'clock in the morning, could be viewed as entering into a mutually beneficial negotiation. They implicitly use the cornerstone of most negotiations in the world: the conditional negotiation phrase: "If... then..."

In this case, the infant is suggesting that, "If you feed me, change me and comfort me then I will go back to sleep and so can you." So there is a mutual benefit in the parent responding.

As we acquire language and cognitive skills in childhood, we enter into more advanced and conscious negotiations with parents and peers, adding a range of tactics to the situation. In our teen years we become more adept and add further to our skill set. The learning process continues into adulthood.

Yet, although we improve through experience, very few of us receive any formal training in negotiation. Upon entering the adult world, we may fail to recognise our daily dealings with those around us as forms of negotiation.

Let us look at the kind of negotiator you are in the following exercise.

Tick five of the following statements with which you agree most strongly:

a) The essence of good negotiating is to drive a hard bargain

b) Negotiation is essentially joint problem-solving

c) The most important thing in negotiation is to maintain a good relationship

d) Both parties should get their needs satisfied

e) A good negotiator sticks to his or her guns

f) In every negotiation there has to be a winner and a loser

g) It is important to avoid unpleasant confrontations

h) I will yield to principle but not to pressure

I) I believe in trusting the 'other party' completely

j) Exploring mutual interests is the key to successful negotiating

k) A successful negotiation means that my interests prevail

l) I believe the most important thing is to maintain harmony and keep the peace

m) Collaboration is the key word

n) Business is business

o) I believe in making concessions to preserve the relationship

Now look at the groupings of letters that follow and circle the ones you ticked above. Write your score in each group.

1. a, e, f, k, n...............total.............

2. b, d, h, j, m.............total............

3. c, g, i, l, o...............total...........

The questionnaire is based on the assumption that in most negotiations every negotiator has two important concerns (further explained in Fisher and Ury's excellent book *Getting to Yes*). The first concern is with the substance or aim of the negotiation and the second is the relationship with the 'other party'. Negotiators vary considerably in the emphasis they place on these two considerations and the shift of emphasis at different stages in the negotiation.

If you scored highest in 1) you are probably a **High Substance/Low** Relationship type of negotiator. This means you place more emphasis on getting what you want rather than preserving the relationship with the other party. You are quite likely to be this kind of negotiator if you are buying a used car or your first flat. You want to get the best price possible and are probably not too concerned about the relationship with the seller – unless you live next door to them!

If you scored highest in 2) you are probably a **High Substance/High Relationship** type. You attach equal importance to both getting what you want and to the relationship. This is the best style of negotiation – someone who sets limits and objectives in order to achieve the best possible outcome, but also someone who cares about the other party and wants the best outcome for him or her as well.

If you scored highest in 3) you are most likely a **Low Substance/High Relationship** type. For you, maintaining the relationship is most important – even if this means accepting less than you really want. Early in our negotiating experience, we are quite likely to be this kind of negotiator. As you gain confidence and learn to prepare in advance, you are less likely to end up with far less than you want or deserve.

Credit: The above exercise is taken from the Negotiating Style Profile developed by Rollin and Christine Glaser.

Negotiation is a structured process with generally six phases:

- Preparation
- Opening the negotiation
- Discussion
- Proposals and bargaining
- Closing the negotiation
- Follow-up

In order to fully understand and apply these six phases, I'd like you to imagine that you are negotiating for a wage or salary increase. This might be for a Saturday job that you have held for over a year, or more importantly in your first job after leaving university or school. Please note that the principles covered below apply to any negotiation – not just a salary increase.

Preparation

I can't emphasise how critical preparation is in any negotiation. To enter a negotiating engagement without thorough prep exposes you to too much risk and too many surprises.

All good negotiators enter into negotiations well prepared. They have identified their objectives, set their priorities, and assessed the other side's position. They have planned their strategy and tactics to achieve the desired result. If the process involves a team, each member has been briefed on the way ahead, and will be able to make a positive contribution to the process.

Firstly, you must determine what you want from the negotiation – what you would consider an ideal outcome. Be bold here. You are negotiating for a salary increase. Think the greatest percentage they could possibly give. Next, you must determine what would be acceptable given the market and economic conditions in your company – this is the figure that you would be OK with and is hopefully not too far off your ideal outcome. Finally you must determine what would make you walk away from the negotiation. In doing this you must explore all your options. A walk-away position might mean leaving your job, so it's important to know how long it might take you to find another one. Michael Donaldson, in his excellent book *Fearless Negotiating,* calls this approach the Wish, Want, Walk.

This is sometimes known as our Best Alternative to a Negotiated Agreement (BATNA).

To identify the BATNA, take the following steps:

- List all the courses of action you could take if negotiations fail

- Consider the consequences of each course of action in terms of your strategy

- Determine the best of these options: this is the BATNA

During the negotiation, you should judge all offers against the BATNA:

- If the offer is better than your BATNA, you are on the 'positive side'

- If the offer is worse than your BATNA, negotiate to close the gap

- If they won't improve the offer, exercise your BATNA.

In the case of your salary increase this might include one of the following options:

1. Asking for another review in three to six months

2. Requesting to be moved to a different job

3. Leaving the organisation and looking for a job elsewhere

Clearly there are some major factors to consider if you exercise the third option. Will I be able to find another job quickly? Do I have enough money to tide me over until I find a new position? Am I likely to miss this job and the team I am working with? Should I just be patient and wait a year? There are many things I can learn from this company and the people I work with.

Secondly, you need to identify trade-offs or options, particularly if you are accepting less than you had hoped for. These might be a later start date for your working day, a new laptop, mobile phone, extra holiday time, flexible working hours, luncheon vouchers, etc. These may well be within the gift of your company and relatively easy for them to provide and will help take the sting out of not achieving your Wish or Want position.

Thirdly, you must identify your own USPs – a term frequently used in selling but equally applicable to you personally. A USP is a Unique Selling Point, or a UVP is your Unique Value Proposition. These USPs or UVPs represent the value you bring to your organisation in terms of expertise, experience, special skills, knowledge, and strengths. You must be prepared to bring these to the table, especially when negotiating for a major promotion or salary increase. Be prepared to answer the questions: "Why should we give you this increase?" or "What contribution do you think you make to this organisation?"

You should prepare these answers in advance and you should also consider other questions or objections which might be raised in the meeting.

You must be very focused in your communication. Speak with brevity and impact and remember to mirror your language with tone of voice and positive body language. This means you enter the negotiation with confidence – back straight, head up, good eye contact, smile and strong handshake. Listen carefully, take notes if you wish and, when you speak, be clear and assured in your message. You can prepare and rehearse this in advance – in fact I strongly encourage you to do so.

Let's look at the following negotiating model:

Entry position: this represents your ideal outcome and what you will ask for ➜ 10% increase

This space is your bargaining area where you will explore the trade-offs and options

Acceptable position: this represents what you will accept ➜ 6% increase

This space is your further bargaining area where you must strongly ask for the options which might be within their gift. The closer you get to 5% the more of these you will want to achieve

Disappointing but will still accept: ➜ 4% increase

Walk away from the negotiation: ➜ less than 4%. This is where you will exercise your BATNA

The next stage in the preparation phase of the process is to examine the likely position of the other party. We should use exactly the same techniques as we have to clarify our own position. Again, if you have a negotiation team, all team members should participate in this activity.

As a starting point, we can prepare a list of our own perceptions of their desired outcomes: our estimate of their wish list. This estimate will form the basis of the questions to be asked at the Discussion Phase, in which the estimate can be validated.

These questions will include:

- What do they want?

- What are they prepared to trade?

- With whom will we be negotiating?

- Will they have the authority to close the deal?

- How will they try to negotiate?

- What might they want from me?

We should identify what we believe is their minimum position. This is the point beyond which a deal ceases to be viable. The next important task is to estimate their priorities in the same manner as we did when setting our own, in the same four categories.

Opening the Organisation

The atmosphere in which the negotiation is set will determine the whole tone of the meeting. If you are responsible for the setting, ensure that it provides an environment conducive to negotiating. The other party should be made to feel welcome.

As we are negotiating for a salary increase, it is highly likely that the other party will open the negotiation. Best practice negotiation dictates that this should be done in a friendly, non-threatening manner in order to set everyone at ease. Remember to enter the room with confidence, smile and shake hands. Thank the other person for the opportunity to meet. You might be offered refreshments. You will certainly be invited to sit down. Avoid slouching in your chair. Sit in the forward half of the seat – 'energy forward', which was described in Chapter 2. When you answer a question or make a point, lean into the desk, table or other person. This shows enthusiasm, energy and interest as opposed to lack of energy and disinterest in the pro-ceedings. Do read Chapter 9 for more information on personal presence.

Discussion

It is increasingly common to conduct negotiations from a dis-tance. Rather than meeting in person, people negotiate over the telephone, or even by an exchange of e-mails. **The best negoti-ations though are face to face.**

A key objective in holding discussions is to establish rapport between the parties and to ascertain what they want and what they are likely to give. It is an opportunity to ask and answer questions. As this is a salary negotiation you are quite likely to be asked the following questions:

- How do you like working here?

- Are you finding your role challenging?

- What do you think you have contributed over the past year?

- What do you think has been your best achievement since you have been in the job?

- Where do you see yourself heading in this organisation?

Active listening

Active listening is a crucial skill in negotiation, particularly in gathering information. Active listening is more than simply listening, nodding and smiling. You should engage with what the other party is saying. For example, we can make comments in such a way that we can secure more information:

"That's interesting, please tell me more"

Or

"Oh! I think I see; perhaps you could explain how that will work in our situation"

Another method of active listening is to 'play back' your understanding of what you have been told. This serves two purposes:

- To confirm your understanding

- To establish a relationship by demonstrating that you are listening and that you really do understand

"So, if I understand you correctly, this means that..."

Asking questions

Asking questions is a key part of negotiation. By asking the right questions you can find out more, clarify information, build good relationships with others and help others think better. No one likes to be lectured, but everyone likes to be asked their opinion – asking questions can be very persuasive.

Let's look at some different types of questions you could ask in a negotiation:

Open questions

Open questions are good for finding out information, getting to the bottom of complex issues, understanding why someone has reacted in a particular way or taken a particular course of action, exploring opinions.

- What…
- What else…
- Why…
- How…
- Tell me more about…
- Can you describe…

Closed questions

Closed questions are useful for eliciting specific information.

- Where do you live?
- What time will you arrive?
- Do you like butter?

Rhetorical questions

Rhetorical questions enable you to use the openness of questions, and engage people, when actually making a statement: "Isn't it a lovely day?"

Reflective questions

These mirror the statements made by the other person, and invite a more open response, for example: "I understand what you mean. I'm just wondering how that would impact the position. What do you think?"

Consequence questions

Such as: "If I were to agree to do this, what effect might it have on your decision?"

One powerful technique in questioning returns us to childhood conditioning. Children are taught that if they ask permission to ask a question, then adults will respond honestly.

"Do you mind if I ask you a question?"

The question is asked as if we are a child asking permission of an adult. It is likely that the person of whom this question is asked will give permission. Also, it is likely that they will then be motivated to answer honestly, and could remove their guard.

Proposals and Bargaining

Having prepared our negotiating position and confirmed or altered it as a result of discussion, we are now set to move to the proposals and bargaining phase. This is where that preparation will be particularly useful as you negotiate your options and try to move them towards your ideal outcome.

Making a proposal is a skill in its own right. Competent negotiators will move easily between conditional and non-conditional proposals, depending upon the relative power and positions of the negotiating parties.

Make sure you clarify offers made during this stage and summarise what has been agreed.

Closing Down the Negotiation

Once we have agreed all the negotiating points it is time to close the negotiation.

This phase creates the most difficulty for many of us, perhaps through our upbringing. Many people do not feel comfortable with the direct approach required in closing a negotiation, i.e. Are you agreeing this increase? Do we have the business? When can we sign the contract? However it is an important skill and you should practise using it.

Many people are good openers in that they can establish good rapport, elicit all of the other side's wants, gain answers to all of their own questions, and so on. However, good closers are much rarer.

Follow-Up

Once your increase has been agreed there will be some fol-low-up actions. This will include a confirmation letter or e-mail from your boss or the HR department. You might also write a note to those in the negotiation thanking them for their time and (hopefully!) for making positive decisions from which you will benefit.

In other types of negotiation, follow-up might include:

- Drawing up a contract or terms of engagement

- Writing a confirmation e-mail

- Arranging further meetings

- Putting together a written document outlining next steps

Negotiating and Body Language

In other chapters in this book we discuss the importance of positive body language. Here are some of the behaviours you should display in a negotiation.

Positive visual behaviour

To show co-operation/friendliness:

- Eye contact at least 50% of the time

- Nodding head, as if in agreement

- Smiling, friendly expression

- Arms and legs uncrossed

- Sitting forward in chair

- Moving closer to the other person

To show confidence:

- Try not to blink rapidly
- Look into the other person's eyes
- Thrust chin forward
- Avoid hand-to-face gestures
- 'Steeple' fingers together
- Hands behind back, if standing
- If sitting, head back and stretch out legs
- Avoid nervous gestures

To show thoughtfulness/listening:

- Look at other person at least 60% of the time
- Tilt your head slightly
- Nod/smile
- Put hand to cheek
- Spectacle wearers put ear-frame to mouth
- Stroke chin or pinch bridge of nose
- Lean forward
- Don't fidget or shuffle

And these are some behaviours to avoid.

Negative Visual Behaviour

These make you appear defensive:

- Not looking at the other person
- Crossing arms and legs
- Clenching hands
- Rubbing eyes, nose or ears
- Leaning away
- Pointing your body towards exit

These make you appear nervous:

- Blinking frequently
- Offering little eye contact
- Licking your lips
- Clearing your throat
- Covering your mouth while speaking
- Constant fidgeting
- Weak handshake

These make you appear bored:

- Staring blankly
- Putting your head in your hands
- Doodling
- Drumming fingers on table
- Tapping feet

- Showing little or no eye contact

- Yawning

- Looking at your watch

These make you appear aggressive:

- Staring too much

- Raising your eyebrows to show disbelief

- Pointing your finger

- Thumping fist on table

- Standing while other person is sitting

The Ten Key Traits of Master Negotiators

Let's consider the key skills that truly effective negotiators bring to the table:

- They keep emotional distance – i.e. they avoid taking the negotiation personally

- They communicate well in terms of knowing when to speak and having the ability to communicate articulately and with impact

- They prepare well

- They empathise with the other party

- They have high integrity

- They are insightful and understand different behaviours

- They have a good deal of patience

- They are flexible and willing to compromise when necessary

- They have stamina

- And finally, they are excellent listeners

These skills can be practised and learnt.

Question: Do you think you possess some of them? Are you willing to develop others?

The Major Negotiating Pitfalls

As someone who has been in many negotiations over the years, I can honestly admit that I have made some very bad mistakes. But the good thing about failing is that you can learn from your errors. Here are some things to avoid in any negotiation:

- Not preparing properly

- Being totally inflexible

- Losing emotional control

- Not focusing on your objectives for the negotiation

- Not listening to the other party

- Communicating in a confusing or rambling manner

- Negotiating with the wrong person – i.e. someone who does not have the authority to make or influence a decision

Final Word

True negotiation only occurs when...

- Two or more parties are actively engaged

- There is a real desire by those involved to reach a productive outcome

- Deals are entered into willingly by all satisfied parties

- The needs, concerns, wants and desires of both parties are addressed

- Both parties have something to offer and gain

- The implications of decisions are carefully considered

- People are willing to move and don't hold to fixed positions

- People listen to each other

- Reasonable demands are made

CASE STUDY

You will undoubtedly have to do a lot of negotiation in your campaign. This might include:

• Negotiating with suppliers – printing, graphics, entertainment, local retailers

• Negotiating with your team regarding roles, responsibilities, timetables, deadlines, etc.

• Negotiating with the senior management team and your school governors in terms of what their expecta-

---

tions are and when you will be in a position to deliver results

Remember to prepare fully for all these negotiations and consider the other party's needs and positions. Remember the better prepared you are and the more you listen, the more successful you will be.

Chapter Summary

I hope that this chapter has demonstrated that negotiation is not a mystic art, but a structured process that can be learned and repeatedly used. The steps and advice given should help you to rediscover innate skills, enhance existing skills, and acquire new ones. These will enable you to build the confidence required to negotiate effectively. By deploying your skills regularly and readily you will find they become a core competence. There is no doubt that being an effective and fair negotiator is a key skill in the workplace.

Further Reading

Six Habits of Merely Effective Negotiators, James Sebenius (*Harvard Business Review,* April 2001)

The 7 Habits of Highly Effective People (*particularly Habits 4,5 and 6),* Stephen Covey (Simon & Schuster, ISBN: 0684858398)

Conflicts, Edward De Bono (Penguin Books,1985, ISBN: 010226842)

The Effective Negotiator, Gerald M Atkinson (Quest Research Publications,1975, ISBN: 0903947150)

Getting to Yes, Roger Fisher and William Ury (Better Business Guides, Hutchison, 1983, ISBN: 0091640717)

Managing Negotiations, Kennedy, Benson and McMillan (Better Business Guides, Hutchison,1987, ISBN: 0091688914)

The Negotiating Game, Chester L Karrass (Crowell,1970, ISBN: 0690003595)

The One Minute Sales Person, S Johnson and L Wilson (Fontana,1986)

The Skills of Negotiating, Bill Scott (Gower Business Skills,1981, ISBN: 07054 05541)

Successful Negotiation, Robert B Maddux (Kogan Page, Better Management Skills, 1988, ISBN: 1850917418)

Negotiation Skills and Strategies, Alan Fowler (Institute of Personnel Management,1990, ISBN: 085292416)

Everything is Negotiable, Gavin Kennedy (Better Business Guides, Hutchison,1982)

International Dimensions of Organizational Behavior, Nancy J Adler (PWS-Kent, 1991, ISBN: 0534922740)

CHAPTER FIVE
Working in Teams

By BRUCE HOVERD

Chapter Overview

One of the areas that we learn an enormous amount about during our time at school, university and early in our work lives is the ability to be an effective member of the many groups that we find ourselves a part of. This means being a contributor, sometimes in quite different ways, as well as a supporter to others. As our contacts widen, it becomes more essential that we make use of the talents around us, to complement our own skills and develop better results collectively. In this way we achieve more than we would, working on our own. In this chapter we will look at the key ingredients of being an effective team member and will consider what makes for a really high-performance team.

Questions:

What is the best team you have been part of? Why was it so successful and enjoyable?

What is a well-known and successful team that you know of? Why this team?

What group currently excites or energises you and others? What do they do that is different to other groups?

What do these three groups or teams have in common?

Now, consider these four very different, yet astonishingly successful teams and groupings…

Manchester United Football Club who over a considerable period have based their success on strong leadership, continually adding new talents and energising each other to dig deep when things got tough.

Diversity, an astonishingly talented and successful street crew, where all the dancers bring something different and they combine to produce incredibly on-point synthesis and continually develop breakthrough moves.

The Vienna Philharmonic, regarded by many musicians as one of the best orchestras in the world over a period of at least 20 years. They always set high standards and practise until they get it right. Critics and music lovers praise their strikingly fresh interpretations of diverse music, often achieved through encouraging the members to experiment and create their own unique interpretations.

The 2012 Olympics Games Makers. In 2012, thousands of people came together from very different backgrounds and life skills to create an Olympic experience none of us will ever forget. Not just the astonishing performers, or Lord Coe's inspiring leadership, it was the Games Makers who stole the show: ordinary people who combined their energy to create an environment that raised everyone's spirits and created an amazing spectacle.

Question: What can we all learn from these widely recognised examples of team success?

Now consider what teamwork means for you and what you need to do to create a really successful team.

- Firstly you will learn new skills, different approaches and additional ways of dealing with situations by observing how differently others work. By being part of any collective you also continuously add to and build your own strengths and repertoire. Consider a group you joined where you have become more effective by picking up on others' ways of working or performing.

- Second, it is only by combining your talents and styles with those of others, that you will be able to produce results of the quality you and others want. Even the best entrepreneurs and business generators rely on the expertise provided by others to turn products and ideas into business solutions and successes. What ideas have you had that others helped you with?

- Third, groups become our prime source of social and personal support, particularly when the pressure is on and situations get tougher. Turning to others we trust is essential when facing dilemmas, dealing with problems and sorting issues. *When did you need the support of others to get through a difficulty or deal with a problem?*

- Finally, the groups that you want to spend time with are those who will provide you with wonderful hours of pleasure, laughter, energy and excitement. There are many times when we all need a 'sanity' check, release tension, share emotional times and celebrate successes. *What do you gain from a group you have been part of that feels positive and energises you?* Many people are not sure what they can do to become a valuable member of the groups they are part of?

The work of Meredith Belbin has provided some powerful insights into the different ways that people contribute within teams. He and others since have observed that the most successful business groups contain members who take on quite distinct roles, as needed. They became more effective as teams when the members recognised the need to exercise a particular role at a certain point in the activities they were working on. We each have a preference for several of these roles, but we also add to the group when we are prepared to step into additional roles that are not necessarily playing to our greatest strengths. These more successful teams also made a point of recognising and showing they valued each other's contribution.

- The most successful teams in all areas have members who display the following characteristics:
  - They use their preferred roles when the team experiences difficulty or runs into a problem. Because these

roles normally represent our strengths, we are likely to be able to add real value, positive action and confidence when situations become difficult.

- They consider the timing of their actions so that they can contribute most when the group needs to make progress or move forward.

- They learn to change their roles according to the situation they are in at any point. If what you are doing is not working, consider what other role may be more productive for you to adopt at that point.

- They give clear signals when they are changing their role through the language they use. Others will understand what you are attempting to do in a role if you tell them, for example, "I've been listening to the discussion and have thought of some different ways we could deal with this issue." This sign-posting is helpful in all contexts. Others are not mind readers! Too often we just state our opinions or what we think, without giving any context or offering clarity about how we reached our conclusions.

- They exercise self-restraint. Only use your role if it will add value, support others or enable progress to be made. Sometimes it's better to be a supportive team member and remain quiet for a period. The best goal scorers in most sports teams wait for an opportunity and seize it when it comes.

- They do not attempt to be all things to all people. We all know people who dominate, have something to say on everything and get involved in as many things as possible. Playing to your strengths as needed is a valuable asset that allows others to take a leadership role, and is part of group sharing and valuing each other's contributions.

– They are clear about which roles they are not going to hold. We learn what we are not particularly good at and allow others the opportunity to exercise their preferred roles in these ways. Usually using less preferred roles may slow up or inhibit group progress.

– They provide opportunities for others. We all learn by being given opportunities to enact our preferred roles. Consider where you can generate opportunities or experiences for others to learn. This also gives you the pleasure of having helped others to develop.

– They make personal sacrifices to achieve team goals. Sometimes we persist in pushing our views or our position on an issue, and this creates tension and frustration. Our egos can prove to be powerful blockers and learning when we need to exercise restraint and allow others to have their way is a powerful piece of personal growth.

Let's look at the eight team roles according to Belbin:

Consider each role and identify those you would say are your current preferences that you use more regularly.

Which characteristics do you associate with?

When do you function best?

Where might you over-use a role?

Who do you recognise as having other roles around you?

1. The Plant

Characteristics	Innovative
	Inventive
	Creative
	Sows the seeds of ideas
	Imaginative
	Unorthodox
	Radical
	Original
	Absorbed in thought
	Clever
	Independent
Functions best	Generating new proposals
	Solving complex or difficult problems
	Recharging a discussion and solutions, when progress is blocked
	Reforming things that need a new perspective
Potential concerns	Independence
	Difficulty communicating ideas
	Introverted
	Impractical
	Reacts strongly to criticism
	Preoccupied
	Timing of sharing ideas can be misplaced

2. The Resource-Investigator

Characteristics	Enthusiastic
	Animated
	Quick off the mark
	Communicative
	Negotiator
	Network
	Develops others' ideas
	Inquisitive
	Thinks on their feet
	Persuasive
	Relaxed
	Gregarious
Functions best	Exploring and creating new opportunities
	Developing external contact
	Reporting back
	Probing
	Keeping up to date
	Representing the group to others
	Acting as an ambassador
Potential concerns	Sociable
	Initial enthusiasm may fade
	Over-optimistic
	Off and running before a decision has been made
	Asks a lot of questions
	Has a lot of avenues to explore
	Restless

3. The Monitor-Evaluator

Characteristics	Serious-minded
	Prudent
	Thinks things over
	Critical thinker
	Makes shrewd judgments
	Takes all factors into account Sober
	Dispassionate
	Sceptical
	Objective
Functions best	Analysing problems
	Evaluating ideas and suggestion
	Developing a strategy
	Making crunch decisions
	Weighing up the pros and cons of options
	Presenting a detached view
Potential concerns	Slow making decisions
	Appear overcritical
	Dry and overserious
	Can block progress
	Can be perceived as lacking drive and energy
	Little sense of urgency

4. The Co-Ordinator

Characteristics	Mature
	Trusting
	Confident
	Delegates easily
	Spots individual talents
	Adopts a broad outlook
	Tackles problems calmly
Functions best	Clarifying and getting others working towards shared goals
	Allocating of resources
	Standing back from the action
	Presenting a worldly view
	Encouraging others to contribute
	Boosting morale
	Making decisions
	Orchestrating
	Facilitating
	Arbitrating
Potential concerns	Can clash with Shapers
	Highly consultative
	Overgenerous to some members of the team
	Delegates and offloads too much
	Can become lazy

May be perceived as manipulative if pushing own agenda

5. The Shaper

Characteristics	Highly motivated
	Needs to achieve results
	Drives strongly
	Challenges
	Competitive
	Argumentative
	Determined
	Provocative
	Hardworking
	Emphatic communicator
Functions best	Pushing others into action
	Sparking life into a team
	Taking unpopular decisions
	Imposing shape and pattern
	Keeping things moving when the group is under pressure
Potential concerns	Aggressive
	Shows strong emotional response
	Lacks interpersonal sensitivity
	Has to win
	Can offend others
	Slave-driver
	Believes him/herself to be right

6. The Implementer

Characteristics	Practical
	Common sense
	Disciplined
	Self-controlled
	Hard worker
	Systematic
	Reliable
	Efficient
	Just gets on with it
Functions best	When has the capacity to apply things
	Doing the things others won't
	Focusing on feasibility and relevance
	Taking reality checks
	Keeping things ticking over
Potential concerns	Lacks spontaneity
	Rigidity/inflexibility
	Locks into detailed tasks
	Can be taken advantage of
	Slow to respond to new possibilities
	Reliant on what has worked in the past

7. The Team Worker

Characteristics	Supportive of others
	Sociable
	Concerned
	Flexible and adaptive
	Perceptive
	Diplomatic
	Sensitive
	Actively
	Listens well
Functions best	Preventing interpersonal problems arising
	Allowing others to contribute
	Lubricating discussions
	Fostering collaboration and team spirit
	Maintaining relationships
	Checking how others are feeling
Potential concerns	Can be indecisive
	Avoids friction and issues
	Rescues others
	Difficult to know where they stand
	Lack of task focus
	Seeks the input and commitment of all
	Can be too accommodating

8. The Completer Finisher

Characteristics	Follows through
	Attends to detail
	Painstaking
	Appears unruffled
	Sets high standards
	Conscientious
	Accurate
Functions best	Where accuracy and attention to detail are needed
	When others are distracted
	Creating urgency
	Meeting schedules
	Ensuring follow-up
	Improving on the final product
	As a quality controller
Potential concerns	Intolerant of informality
	Tackles all tasks
	Introversion
	Internally anxious and worriedWorries unduly
	Fussy

WHY DO TEAMS MALFUNCTION AND FAIL?

WHAT WILL INDICATE POSITIVE FUNCTIONING AND SUCCESS?

A good place to start understanding what goes wrong is by looking at those teams who struggle in sport; a good example would be those who are relegated from the FA Premiership each year. Patrick Lencioni, a team effectiveness expert, has identified the five most common areas where teams come unstuck. We can all look at teams we are part of and identify where specific issues are occurring and what we can do to deal with these.

1. Lack of trust

You will be able to identify when people in your teams trust each other by the levels of:

- Admitting when they have made mistakes, taking responsibility for doing something about errors and accepting apologies

- Asking for and offering help

- Giving straight feedback

- Concentrating on important issues

- Wanting to spend time together

2. Fear of conflict

This does not exist where:

- Lively discussions occur

- Everyone is contributing

- There is regular exploring of alternative solutions and real problems are solved quickly

- It feels easy to express concerns

3. Lack of commitment

Signs of a committed team are:

- Having a clear sense of direction and priorities

- Sharing goals

- Learning from mistakes

- Taking advantage of opportunities

- Changing direction when change is needed

- Focusing on moving forward

4. Avoidance of responsibility

A team that takes responsibility seriously:

- Applies positive pressure to improve when performance is poor

- Identifies where the problems exist

- Questions the validity of certain approaches

- Shows respect for the achievement of high quality work and consistently high standards

- Understands what each other is doing and why

5. Lack of attention to results and outcomes

Where teams focus on results, you will notice:

- Attention to getting the key things right

- Understanding what success will be like

- Aiming high and concentrating on achieving consistently good results

- Signs of growth planning and action that will lead to growth or positive change

- Energy concentrated on winning ahead of competitors

Consider several teams you are currently involved with and identify which of these indicators are true for the state that your teams are in.

What currently happens in these groups positively/negatively?

What does this model suggest you need to do as a group to improve your team performance and sustain high quality results?

Given the difficulties that teams can experience, it is also important for you to consider what you personally can do when things are not working in teams and when there are very different perceptions or ideas. Our research indicates that the most common behaviours that promote team effectiveness, when improvement is needed, are:

BEING CURIOUS and OBSERVING. Take an interest in what others are saying, what they are doing and what is happening between individuals or amongst the group as a whole. You will learn something about what you or others can do to change the situation!

IDENTIFYING THE IMPORTANT INFORMATION. Accept the opinions of others as adding to the store of information that will help to create the best discussions and decisions. Attempt to identify the best ideas that will achieve the outcomes you want.

ACTIVELY LISTENING. Find out what is really being said and, if you don't understand, explore or enquire. What is not being said? You may be valued more for giving full attention and reflecting your understanding rather than adding new thinking, or saying too much.

PROVIDING CLARITY. If you have something to say, it is worth being as concise, precise and to-the-point as possible. Most language becomes confusing if padding, waffle and jargon are used.

EXPLAINING YOUR AND OTHERS' THINKING. Explain or ask for the context and how you or they have reached the opinion or conclusion. Others are not mind readers!

PROVIDING SIGNPOSTS. For example, "my proposal", "the benefits of that will be", "having listened to everyone, I have concluded", "let me summarise".

MOVING ON. Learn when it is time to finish a discussion, make a decision, focus on the plan and take action. Avoid that common business disease 'analysis paralysis'!

FOCUSING. Pay attention to those things which are distracting you and others from playing a full part in the discussion such as bias, dislike, laziness, boredom or tonight's dinner. Concentrate on what you are all there to achieve and how it can best be done.

TOUGH TALKING. When it needs to be said, say it. Issues and concerns can only be resolved if voiced first. A useful way of doing this is to use 'we' language and base it on an observation of what is not working – for example, "We keep going over the same points and we need to make a decision now".

CASE STUDY

USING YOUR UNDERSTANDING OF SUCCESSFUL TEAMS TO POSITIVELY WORK TOGETHER ON YOUR CAMPAIGN

It will make an enormous difference to the quality of the work you produce if you take some time to consider how you work together as a group and review this throughout the process.

These six areas will be critical to your success and will enhance the relationships that you build:

1) **Ensure that everyone is working on the same page.** Early in your task, you need to clarify your purpose for undertaking this activity and ensure that everyone agrees. Also check throughout the process that everyone understands where you are en route to completion. If there are too many different activities happening at once, members of the team can become focused on their own activity and lose sight of what you as a group are working to accomplish overall.

2) **Share objectives.** Different group members will have different ideas about which outcomes will indicate a successful result. An opportunity needs to be provided early in the campaign to identify all the outcomes that individuals want and decide, given your purpose, what specific outcomes are most important for you to aim at and to achieve. What do you personally want to see this group achieve?

3) **Delegate roles.** The best teams, as we have already identified, ensure that different people take on the

different roles that are needed throughout a project. It is also essential that individuals get an opportunity to play to their strengths wherever possible. The exception to this occurs when individuals are clear that they wish to take on a different role in order to learn ways of performing differently and building additional skills. When this happens, the team needs to encourage the person as they will not necessarily be perfect straightaway and will need support. With practice and opportunities they will become more skilful. Referring to the earlier content on Belbin team roles, which of these will play to your strengths?

4) **Build and maintain motivation.** Individuals will lose motivation if they are not involved, not supported, and only carrying out 'basic' tasks. Each person is most likely to be energised, involved and contributing if you as a group ensure and check that their level of involvement and inclusion is working for them. Notice when people have withdrawn, look disinterested, seem to be negative or are not engaged with what is happening. Support and encourage them, and listen to what they think. What about this task will ensure that you remain motivated?

5) **Deal with problems.** Problems arise in all groups and are not easy to predict, so everyone needs to be on the lookout for the signs that indicate something is not right and needs to be responded to. Watch out for loss of focus, activities taking longer than expected, dissatisfaction with what is occurring, and a sense of being stuck or a lack of progress. When these things happen, it is best to stop the process and identify what is occurring

and what needs to change in the way you are working. Alternatively the leaders of the group may take time out to discuss what is happening and make proposals to the group about improving or solving the problem. Knowing the people in your group, where are problems likely to occur? When this happens, what do you and others normally do to resolve the difficulties?

6) **Overcoming challenges.** As you progress, situations will occur that you have not dealt with before, or they seem to generate blocks or mountains to climb. This can halt a group's progress or raise concerns for some members. When this happens, you as a group need to find the best ways of reassuring individuals and encouraging them to stick with what is happening and work through it. Peer encouragement to others to "have a go", change roles, "raise your game", and focus on the positives, can be very powerful. What about this task is likely to be challenging for you and others? How do you normally deal positively with the challenges you face?

Questions:

From this chapter about team working, what have you decided you will do differently or develop to increase your effectiveness as a team member and influencer?

What do you now understand about the most effective teams that will lead you to develop your skills?

The team role you most want to develop is?

What opportunities will you have in the next year that will support you in developing this role?

How positively are the teams which you are currently a part of performing and where should the team improve?

What can you do more of when your teams are not working as well as they might?

Chapter Summary

You can learn an enormous amount from the effective teams you have been part of and what you already know about the highly successful teams you have observed in all manner of fields. What do they do differently?

The benefit of taking part and contributing to the teams you are or will be part of is crystal clear. It is these teams that will provide you with future opportunities to learn new skills, develop your creativity, provide support for you when you need it and establish a place to celebrate success.

Considering your team roles allows you to focus on becoming involved in the most appropriate activities, at the right times. Playing to your team role strengths is likely to increase the level of successful outcomes that you achieve with others.

Paying attention to what you and others are doing when your team is not working effectively, will lead you to identify what you and others need to do to change the situation. Understanding the indicators of poor performing teams will help you and your teams to identify areas for improvement.

Finally, by building your team skills, you will take a stronger role in leading and facilitating the progress of the teams you are in and increasing your impact. Increasingly, employers look at how people work with others and what they have achieved in groups. This has become a must if you want to get certain roles and stand out from the crowd.

In the next chapter we will look at some important skills that all good team players need to have: good time management and the ability to manage pressure.

Further Reading

Effective Teambuilding: How to Make a Winning Team, John Adair (Pan, 2009)

The Wisdom of Teams (explores the benefits of teams and ways they can move towards achieving high performance), Jon R Katzenbach and Douglas K Smith, (McGraw-Hill, 1993)

The Five Dysfunctions of a Team (what is at the heart of teams that struggle and ways of building a cohesive team, Patrick Lencioni (Jossey-Bass, 2002)

Fish!: A Remarkable Way to Boost Morale and Improve Results (a story about a manager who transforms an unenthusiasic and unhelpful department into an effective team), Stephen C Lundin, Harry Paul and John Christensen (Hodder & Stoughton, 2000)

Me Myself and My Team: How to Become an Effective Team Player Using NLP, Angus McLeod (Crown House, 2006)

Leading Your Team: How to Set Goals, Measure Performance and Reward Talent, Graham Yemm (The FT Guides, Pearson, 2012)

CHAPTER SIX
Time and Stress Management

By BRUCE HOVERD and DR GAIL DAVIES with CAROLINE HOPKINS

Chapter Overview

In this chapter we will look at two important areas of university and work life – managing your time effectively and dealing with stress. As exams and other deadlines approach, it is essential that you plan your work to make sure that everything gets done in a timely way and that you do not leave everything to the last minute. It is also important to know where to get support, when to delegate and how to use the proper resources to get the job done. When we have a lot to do and important deadlines are looming, we can often find ourselves under tremendous pressure. Pressure is not a bad thing as it can help you focus as well as marshal your energies towards a goal, but too much pressure can lead to stress which in turn can lead to mental and physical health problems. Not a good thing at all!

Leadership and Time Management

In Chapter 1 we covered some key leadership traits – good time management is one of them. The most effective leaders are those who manage their time and organise their workload well. In reality the role is split between maintenance and development activities, i.e. between the routine administration that is required and the developmental activities that move people and projects forward. The effective leader will recognise the potential conflict in the role and will be able to ensure that tasks are prioritised and work is allocated between maintenance and development.

Managing time as a resource

Most people find themselves with too much to do and not enough time to do it or are bored with time on their hands. Given that we only have a finite amount of time available, we need to treat it as a precious commodity. This is particularly true when we have valuable goals to achieve, important tasks to complete, and significant situations to manage. When time has been used we don't get it back, so how you use the time you have becomes even more critical.

To best manage your time, you first need to understand where it goes and how productively you use it. Reflect on your favourite 'time stealers', which you may well recognise from the list below:

Mark those that you know take away your valuable time

- Longer periods of sleep than you need

- Absorption in a range of technology-based activity

- The demands of others

- Distractions around you

- Inane or 'trivial' social interaction

- Repetitive basic everyday activities

- Correcting mistakes you and others have made

- Interruptions

- Attempting to perform a number of jobs at once

- Carrying out tasks others could do

- Engaging in negative behaviour with others

- Displacement activity (i.e. anything that means you don't have to do a task you don't like)

The more you experience these time stealers, the more likely it is that you will be rushed into frantic undertaking and hasty completion of other 'more essential' activities.

How, therefore, can you provide as much time as possible to make conscious choices about what you do and allow sufficient time to think through problems and make decisions in a clear way?

Get it right first time

By focusing on the job at hand and maintaining concentration and focus, it is likely that you will make fewer errors, and avoid having to repeat what you have already done. Notice what distracts you or draws your attention away from the job you are engaged in. How can you get back on track?

Develop a plan

At least start your week with a plan that will remind you of what you intend to achieve and help you to focus on the important 'stuff'. Base this plan on what you will have done and by when. Create approximate timings for each of your essential and important tasks then build flexibility into the plan to allow for the unexpected. Rushing from one activity to another will never put you into the best state to deal with a heavy workload, solve problems, and manage difficult situations. Allowing thinking time within your plan means you will be better prepared and able to concentrate more easily.

One job at a time

Many people think they can multitask but you will notice that some of the activity gets short changed when you attempt to do this. If it is important, then give your full, focused attention to it. When you are out with others, do you find it irritating when they're constantly ignoring you to deal with texts, tweeting or using other communication tools? By paying more attention to what other people are doing, you will learn more, notice changes around you and show them that you value their time.

Learn to say no

Are you someone who will take on almost anything others ask of you? If so, you must stop accepting some of what appear to be 'delegated' or 'requested' tasks. The more you take on, the less time you will have to do a good job with the things that are important to you. You will find that most people respect you more if you are honest about what you are able to do at any point. It's so easy to slip into becoming the 'doormat' who others take advantage of.

Learning to negotiate about what is possible and realistic is an essential business and life skill. Develop the positive habit of checking out how important and urgent something really is before you agree to take it on.

Seek closure before moving on

It makes sense to finish one task or reach a point where you can easily put something aside, before you begin something else. If you are juggling a number of unfinished activities, your attention will be deflected and it may mean you don't do any of the tasks well, make more mistakes and take poor decisions. Taking ten minutes now to finish off an important job will give you extra focused time later.

Interrupt me at your peril!

I have found that it is helpful to let others know when I am busy, need to shut myself away, or must deal with a situation or finish activities. If we don't give clear messages and signals to others, they will think it is okay to interrupt when they want. Be firm about the time being right for you!

What matters to you?

The clearer you are about what is important in your life and work at any point, the easier it is to decide what you do, how much you take on and what you agree to support others with. If you are in doubt about whether something is a priority, ask yourself and others why it is important and when it really needs to be done.

Time as a resource in your projects and major tasks

We recommend you follow these six group rules in your project work

- Stop when you have done enough analysis, make a clear decision and then move quickly into action

- Divide activities into sub-group tasks whenever possible, especially when you do not need to be involved together as a whole group

- Display your plan so everyone is aware of the targets and time limits

- Allow sufficient time for final preparation to present your ideas and communicate with others

- Allocate someone to have specific responsibility for monitoring and managing time

- If you find yourself short of time, ask for help. If you have time on your hands, look for others who need your input or support

Key point: **You cannot create more time, you can only use the time you have more effectively.**

Let's take a look at the following chart and decide what percentage of time should be spent in each quadrant:

Prioritisation Chart	
Quadrant 1 Urgent & Important	**Quadrant 2** Urgent & Not Important
Quadrant 3 Not Urgent & Important	**Quadrant 4** Not Urgent & Not Important

Activities that are important and urgent include emergencies, complaints, crises, customer demands, tasks or projects that are due, meetings, appointments, staff problems, reports, and submissions. Time management experts suggest that you should spend no more than 15% of your time in this area.

Activities that are important but not urgent are ones which are crucial to your success. They include planning, preparation, scheduling, research, investigation, designing, testing, networking and relationship building, thinking, creating, modelling, developing systems and processes, and developing strategies. You should be spending at least 50 - 60% of your time in this area.

Activities that are not important but seem urgent are ones that include trivial requests from other people, apparent emergencies, minor interruptions and distractions, misunderstandings, and pointless routines or activities. Again, time management experts suggest that you should spend no more than 15% of your time in this area.

Activities that are not important and not urgent are those that include computer games, surfing the internet, lots of coffee breaks, social chats, daydreaming, taking personal phone calls, or reading irrelevant material. The less of your time in this area the better – probably about 10%.

Those experts say a lot of time is wasted on those 'comforting' non-urgent, non-important activities while very little time is spent on important but non-urgent activities that could actually make the biggest difference to a person's success.

Improving Concentration

How many times have you sat at your desk and tried to focus on a task, only to find that your mind is wandering? Despite your best intentions, you just can't concentrate. We've all been in this familiar, frustrating situation, and it's something that can really undermine your performance.

Here are some tips from Mind Tools (www.mindtools.com) to improve your concentration and reduce your daily distractions. This is further covered later in this book in the excellent chapter on memory and revision.

Environment

Your personal work environment plays a large role in your ability to concentrate. The more comfortable and welcoming your environment is, the easier it will likely be for you to stay there and focus.

Here are some ideas for improving your physical environment:

- **Make sure you're comfortable**. Start by ensuring that your chair and desk are at the right height for you to work comfortably. If your chair is too high or your desk is too low, you'll be uncomfortable, and you'll be tempted to use this as an excuse to get up and walk away.

- **Put up pictures**. Viewing a natural scene or watching wildlife can help improve concentration. If you're able to put up pictures in your office or work area, then choose landscapes or natural images that you enjoy. This can help your focus, especially if you can see the pictures from your desk.

- **Shut out distractions as much as possible**. Listening to music can help, especially if it's instrumental music. Some people even use noise machines in their offices – these produce a steady 'white noise' like ocean waves or falling rain. This background noise can drown out other noise, helping you focus better and ignore distractions. However, do make sure you are the type of person who works well with background music playing. Some of us must have complete silence to concentrate properly.

Nutrition

Follow some simple nutritional tips:

- **Drink water**. Many of us don't think about drinking water while we're at work, yet dehydration can make us feel tired, irritable, slow, or even sick. When our brains don't have enough fluid, they can't operate at peak performance. Staying hydrated is an easy way to help improve your concentration during the day.

- **Eat breakfast** – Start your day with a healthy breakfast. It's much harder to concentrate when you're hungry, so eat a well-balanced meal before you go to work. You can also help your concentration throughout the day by keeping healthy snacks at your desk. Almonds, whole-grain crackers, fresh fruit and vegetables are good choices.

- **Get up and move around**. Do you walk around during the day? If you're like many people, you probably don't move around enough. Research has shown that regular walking can help increase your focus during the day.

Mind set

Constant distractions, and the low productivity that comes with them, have become so commonplace in today's offices that doctors have even given it a name: Attention Deficit Disorder or ADD. And they say that entire organisations can suffer from it.

Follow some of these guidelines to help focus your mind:

- **Set aside time to deal with worries**. Many of us have trouble concentrating during the day because we're constantly worrying about other things. It could be an approaching deadline for a project you haven't started, a fellow student who's causing problems, or just the amount of work you have to cope with – exam revision, class projects, etc. If you find yourself distracted by worries, then note these down so that you don't need to hold them in your mind. Then schedule time to deal with these issues.

- **Focus on one task at a time**. It can be much harder to focus if you take minibreaks (15–30 seconds) to answer e-mails, send text messages, or take quick phone calls. Some researchers believe that it can take up to 15 minutes for us to regain complete focus after a distraction.

- **Switch between high- and low-attention tasks**. This can give your brain a rest after heavy concentration. For instance, if you spend two hours working on exam revision, you'll probably feel tired afterward. You can recharge your energy by working on a low-attention task, like sorting your notes, for 15 minutes before going back to your revision.

- **Prioritise**. Having too much to do can be distracting, and this sometimes causes procrastination. Or, you may quickly jump from task to task creating the illusion of work but, in reality, you're not accomplishing very much. If you're not sure which tasks to start or which are most important, take 10 or 15 minutes to prioritise your to-do list.

- **Take short breaks**. We can be masters at focusing, but eventually we're going to need a break. Our minds can struggle to focus intensely on tasks for eight hours a day. This is where it can be better to divide your work into one-hour segments, with a five to ten minute break between tasks. This short break will allow your mind to rest before focusing again.

- **Do your hardest tasks when you're most alert**. This will help you maximise your concentration.

- **Promise yourself a reward**. For instance, make a rule that if you focus intensively for 45 minutes on one task, you can take a break to get a cup of coffee or eat a bar of chocolate when you're done. Little 'self-rewards' can often be great motivators.

Now let's move on to discuss stress management.

Are You Dealing With and Overcoming the Pressures and Stressors You Face?

In a world that has become increasingly fast paced, demanding and with high expectations of quality performance, most people are experiencing higher levels of stress. How true is this for you and your friends? Do you notice yourself being more worried, anxious, struggling to cope or feeling unwell on a regular basis? If so, you can begin to reduce these elements by first recognising the signs, then identifying the causes of the pressure you face and assessing how serious these indicators are.

Some of the main causes of stress in younger people *Circle those that you recognise in yourself*	
Fear of poor performance in examinations	
Presenting in front of others	
Difficult relationships with parents/other adults	
Undertaking major events, e.g. concerts, sporting occasions	
Loss of confidence from having done something poorly	
Changes in a close relationship	
Trauma from a big event, e.g. a death, accident, parental break-up	
Important key signs of stress	
On-going ill health	
Being overcritical of yourself and others	
Low energy	
Lack of confidence in social situations	
Changeable moods and emotions	
Withdrawal from others	

Questions: What is the effect on you? How often are you affected by them?

So what can you do when you recognise you may be affected by pressure situations?

Here are some of the best ways to influence the levels of pressure you are experiencing:

Change your thinking

So much of the pressure that we face is heightened by our own thinking concerning the situations and people involved. If you are concerned about exams, e.g. "If I fail it will be a complete disaster", you can replace the negative thoughts with positive ones, e.g. "I will do the best I can with my current knowledge" or "others will support me with this". Once you have confirmed this to be true, you will put your energy into achieving what you can do rather than what you believe you cannot.

Ensure that you have the support you need around you

When you face pressure situations you will need the best people you know to provide greater support, honesty, understanding and reassurance to help you get through the tough times.

Who do you trust and know will support you?

Who can you build your relationship with, so they will respond when you ask for their help?

Some people do not find it easy to ask for help. It is the most significant step you can take in letting others know what you need from them and building great relationships based on mutual trust. They know how to help us best!

Put in the focused effort needed

Under pressure you will often find yourself distracted, unable to concentrate and more forgetful. At these times you need to put in place some structure, allocate enough time and work to a plan. Working in short bursts, in an environment where you can concentrate, can be useful. Doing things in a more organised way and sticking to your plan will help you do this.

Set yourself some goals

We all know that we are at our best when we have something to strive for, especially something we really want. If you find yourself lost, confused or uncertain, having a challenging goal that is important to you will push you to channel your energy into achievement and making progress.

Get into a positive state of mind

Many people break through pressure and prevent stress by putting themselves in environments, as often as possible, that will improve their mental and emotional state. Ask yourself the following:

- In what situations do you operate at your best?

- When do you feel most positive?

- Who and what makes you laugh?

- What have been wonderful times or situations, when you experienced great fun, thrills and delight?

Go back to these places when situations seem dark or unfriendly.

Managing Your Time Mindfully and Working Under Pressure

You may have heard or read about Mindfulness which is becoming increasingly popular as a way of managing stress and focusing your energies and your thoughts. Being aware of managing your time is a skill which will help you to take control. It will give you the space to work under pressure and be your best. Let's look at some case studies which are excellent examples of Mindfulness.

CASE STUDY ONE

Frances was beginning to feel the rising panic in the pit of her stomach again and had those usual thoughts of not being able to cope. She sensed that it was because she had not planned her revision timetable and was in denial that the exams were only weeks away. She was aware that she had to do something and headed for the stationery shop. As she was paying she felt her shoulders relax and had a new spring in her step as she walked home. Sitting at her desk, Frances felt slightly geeky at the pleasure of feeling in control as she stuck her new revision plan on the wall. Noticing that she had a big smile on her face, she thought how come something as simple as planning her timetable can make her feel so much better?

The reason for this was that she was using her **Sensory Perceptual Mind**, which involves processing signals from the senses including what's going on inside the body. However, we rarely tune into this in everyday life, spending most of our time in our heads 'thinking'. When you notice that you have a knot in your stomach and feel overwhelmed, that is your body trying to tell you something. It is smart to be listening out for these signals, as your body is ahead of your brain. You can do this by taking a pause and checking in with yourself at several regular times during the day. What is going on right now? What are my senses telling me? What are my tensions?

The 'thinking' mind is extremely useful but we have a tendency to overuse it to try to solve everything and we believe everything it tells us. This means we can get caught up in its storytelling, which often features the same old stories "I'm useless at this" or "Things never go right for me". This is particularly powerful when we are feeling stressed. When you catch yourself getting hooked up in these stories, try visualising putting distracting thoughts on a cloud and letting them pass overhead.

Summary and Practice

Consciously **slow down** and **PAUSE** several times in the day.

Practise tuning in to what is going on inside your body using your **Sensory Perceptive Mind.** See it as a dashboard of what is happening around you. Notice any warning signals that flash up. What is going on?

Notice when your 'thinking' mind is being unhelpful and engaged in storytelling. Learn to refocus and pay attention to important tasks. You can do this by taking a simple Mindfulness practice that trains your brain to pay attention where you want it to.

Example: deliberately take your focus of attention to the tip of your nose. Keep your attention there and notice when your mind wanders off. Each time it does, return your focus of attention back to the tip of your nose. You may like to explore any sensations you find here such as the breath moving in and out, wanting to sneeze or wanting to scratch an itch. Can you notice this and not react?

OK, so you have learnt how to manage time mindfully. How about those other moments of pressure when you freeze or just want to run away and hide rather than dealing with them?

CASE STUDY TWO

Joe is thinking about his biology exam last summer and worrying about how he is going to get through his next exams as the same thing might happen again. He becomes sweaty and feels sick, as he recalls the moment when his brain froze and he couldn't think of the answers, even though he had revised thoroughly. He dwells on this and becomes really stressed, not able to sleep at night or concentrate in class. He notices he is becoming irritable and unable to enjoy anything like he used to.

Joe realised that subconsciously he was going into panic mode which is when your body freezes and either gets ready to fight or run away. This is how we are programmed to react to threatening situations and stems from when we needed it for survival – for example when encountering a man-eating tiger! Of course this doesn't happen anymore, but our bodies can't tell the difference. It sets off a cascade of reactions in the body which get our heart pumping faster and all our resources, like memory recall and creativity, shut down so we can be on high alert. We continue to remain on high alert the more we panic and we feel trapped in an exhausting worry cycle.

However, it doesn't have to be this way. We have the option to switch this reaction off. Just by becoming aware that he is getting into panic mode, Joe can choose to take a breathing exercise which will enable him to gain control and calm down.

Notice when you are beginning to feel panicky by picking up on the signs in your body like sweaty palms or your heart beating faster.

STOP and Do a Three-Step Breathing Exercise

Standing up or sitting down, feel your feet on the floor and 'ground' yourself. You may also like to close your eyes if it is comfortable to do so.

Step one

Take a moment to notice what being panicky feels like. What thoughts are coming in to your head and what sensations are going on in your body. Do you feel a knot or tension anywhere in your body?

Step two

Focus on your breath. Taking your attention to your abdomen, see if you can notice the rise and fall as the breath comes in and out of the body (you might like to rest your hand there if it helps). Stay here for a few breaths.

Step three

Expand your attention to the subtle movement of the breath throughout your whole body. Be aware of your posture, where you are sitting or standing and facial expression.

Now open your eyes if they have been closed.

If you feel it would be helpful to be guided through this practice, go to www.mindfulnessatwork.com website and you can get a free download.

The science shows that by practising Mindfulness practices for just ten minutes a day you can change the brain. In doing this you will have better focus and concentration and will be able to learn better. You will be less likely to be hijacked by your emotions, which will mean you will be less panicky and better able to deal with challenges.

CASE STUDY

Let's now return to our main case study, which will certainly require excellent time management as well as the ability to cope well with pressure. How will you deal with

---

the pressures that you and others are facing when you undertake a project such as the sixth form campaign?

Remind yourself and others, as you encounter difficulty and become anxious, to:

• Look out for others under pressure

• Ask for help when you need it

• Translate negative thinking into what can be done and achieved

• Go back to your goals and objectives when you get stuck

• Keep going when pressure builds up, you will break through difficulties and concerns

• Remember to tune into your sensory perceptive mind and do your breathing exercises

In terms of time management, it is critical that the campaign team leader puts together an action plan identifying timings, deadlines and who is responsible for what. There should be regular reporting within the team and any deadlines which look like they might be missed need to be flagged up in advance.

Final Word

In closing we have listed some useful time management tools:

DIARIES. Make sure you have just **one** diary rather than one for school or work and one for personal/social.

- CALENDARS

- WALL CHARTS AND TIMETABLES

- PAPER-BASED ORGANISERS

- PDAs

- MS OUTLOOK

- GOAL-SETTING SOFTWARE SUCH AS GOALPRO 2010

- GOOD FILING SYSTEM

- ROLODEX OR CARD FILES

- CONTACT DATABASE

- INTERNET AND INTRANET

- KNOWLEDGE MANAGEMENT SYSTEMS

- GOOGLE DESKTOP SEARCH

- BRING FORWARD FILE. This is a very useful time management tool. Buy a concertina file and label each partition with a day of the week or month of the year. Pop memory joggers, documents or actions which need to be accomplished on that day or in that month. Check it daily or monthly.

Chapter Summary

In this chapter we have examined the key elements of good time management and you have been given some useful tools and techniques to help you manage your time as effectively as possible. We have looked at barriers to good time management and considered on what sorts of activities you should be spending most of your time. We have also looked at stress management and ways to minimise stress. In particular, we have discussed the importance of being mindful and looked at some specific Mindfulness exercises. Now we turn our attention to the subject of money management – so engage the brain, sit back and enjoy!

Further Reading

Check out a useful web site: www.mindtools.com

And another: www.mind-lab.com

Conquer Your Stress, Cary L Cooper and Stephen Palmer (IPD 2000)

Fit for the Fast Track, Juliette and Michael McGannon (Prentice Hall, 2002)

59 Minutes to a Calmer Life, Paul McGee (Go MAD Books, 2001)

Control Stress: Stop Worrying and Feel Good Now!, Paul McKenna (Transworld, 2009)

Stress Proof Your Life; 52 Brilliant Ideas for Taking Control, Elisabeth Wilson (The Infinite Ideas Company, 2007)

Brilliant Time Management, Mike Clayton (Pearson, 2011)

Time Management for Dummies, Clare Evans (John Wiley, 2008)

Do it Tomorrow and Other Secrets of Time Management, Mark Forster (Hodder & Stoughton, 2006)

Never Check E-Mail in the Morning, Julie Morgenstern (Fireside, 2004)

CHAPTER SEVEN
Managing Your Money

By ANGUS CATER

Chapter Overview

Please focus well on this chapter – it could save you a lot of money! Our guest contributor and financial expert, **Angus Cater**, will give you some excellent tips and tools for developing good money habits. He will discuss the importance of financial planning and budgeting and will help you address the important question of how much money you will need for university. This chapter also covers important aspects of managing money which will serve you well after university such as pensions, mortgages, insurance and your relationship with your bank.

How a Few Simple Good Money Habits Can Change Your Life

When I was six years old, I wanted a wristwatch. My parents, who were well off, did not go out and buy me a watch, but suggested that I save for it. I therefore started putting aside pennies, sixpences and shillings and, after what seemed a very long time (in reality about six months) of counting my pennies, I collected all my coins together and went up to the watch shop with my mum. It was a seminal moment and instructional for us all in this highly consumerist society in which we live.

LESSON 1

If you want something – a watch or an education – plan and budget for it.

LESSON 2

Accept and enjoy the pleasure of delayed gratification. Avoid impulse purchases.

LESSON 3

Understand that, unless you are very rich, you cannot have it all. You have to make choices. And even if you are very rich, you really shouldn't have it all.

Planning and Budgeting

The concept is easy – the application a little less so! It is January and you need £1,000 to go on holiday next August. How do you ensure you have enough money to:

1. Pay the deposit
2. Pay for the holiday and...
3. Have enough spending money so you don't have to go to bed with a book at ten 'o clock each night!

Firstly, where is the money to come from?

- Christmas and birthday money - £100

- Holiday job - £500

- Working in a bar during the university term - £300

- Nice parents - £100

This is all very well but what about all your other living costs and how can we put it all together in a plan or a budget?

Steps to easy budgeting

1. Make a table or, ideally, an Excel spread sheet.

2. Put all your anticipated income over the period into the appropriate slot: for example if you anticipate earning £900 from your holiday job during April, put £900 in the income section for April.

3. Try and anticipate all your monthly expenditure. Be realistic.

	January	February	March	April	May	June	July	August
Opening bank balance	-100	-285	-320	155	610	475	-425	195
Income								
Presents				100				
Holiday job				900			900	350
Bar job	150	200	200		200	200		
M&D								100
Student loan	500	500	500	500	500	500		
Overdraft								
Total	**650**	**700**	**700**	**1500**	**700**	**200**	**900**	**450**
Expenditure								
Elec, Gas etc	15	15	15	15	15			
Food	200	200		200	200			
Socialising	120	120	120	120	200	100	100	50
Travel	30	30	30	30	50	30	30	30
Rent	300	300	300	300	300			
Clothes/toiletries	70	70	70	70	70	70	150	200
Holiday	100					900		250
Total	**835**	**735**	**535**	**735**	**835**	**1100**	**280**	**530**
Closing balance	-285	-320	-155	610	475	-425	195	115

The actual numbers in the example above are not really important and they make some fundamental assumptions: a) that you
have not already spent all your student loan, b) that you live at
home and do not have to pay for food during the holidays, c)
that your last payment of rent is May and not August, and so
on. The crucial point is that you have a plan which you will
want to make as accurate as possible so that you can achieve

your desired result. You will have noted how important that holiday job is to achieve your objectives.

Getting Your Head Around the Cost of University

The average student on a three-year degree course will leave university with around £50,000 of debt. £27,000 of this will be for your fees and the balance for living expenses. Your first task should be to minimise the cost. This could be done in a number of ways:

a) Do I really want to go to university or am I just following the crowd? If you are not particularly academic or motivated you could be better off getting qualifications 'on the job'. Apprenticeships are available and many firms have restarted their 18+ entry. It is a fact that many students either drop out after a year or two at university or finish up with a poor degree in a subject that is not respected by employers. Very many successful business people have had prosperous careers that did not start with university.

b) Consider doing a two-year intensive degree at the following universities: Staffordshire, Buckingham, Greenwich, London School of Commerce and Plymouth. The cost of your degree could come down to £35,000 and the third year could be spent in a job with a salary.

c) Investigate distance learning. The Open University is the UK's leading proponent but there are many overseas universities offering distance learning courses.

d) Research your course at an overseas university. For example the University of Maastricht recruits from the UK and American universities have substantial endowments to help with fees.

e) Research the many scholarships and bursaries available. There is a huge variety according to the course, your particular strength, or your family's financial position. Read the *Educational Grants Directory, The Grants Register, Directory of Grant Making Trusts and the Charities Digest.*

f) Think about living at home. It may be less exciting but it will save money.

g) Plan to work during the holidays and be the first to research and apply for jobs on campus during term time.

h) Obtain sponsorship from a company that recruits from your specialism. Organisations are keen to recruit the best students and it is an opportunity for you to get to know them and vice versa. It could also transform your finances with holiday work and takes away the worry about getting a job after university.

i) Stay in university accommodation for as long as possible. Again, it may be less exciting than sharing a house but it will be cheaper.

j) Budget really carefully and stick to it. I will talk about bank accounts shortly.

Once you are committed to university, stop worrying about the debt. Repayment of student loans is geared to what you earn. You pay nothing at all until after you leave university and your income reaches £21,000 per annum. Thereafter your repayments equal approximately 9% of your salary, so someone earning £27,000 a year will have an approximate monthly salary of £2,250 (before tax and national insurance) and will pay £45 a month. Not a fortune. Even if you earn £50,000 a year (£4,166 per month) the repayment will only be £217.50. If you stop earning you stop repaying and if the whole debt is not repaid after 30 years it is cancelled. This is fair – particularly as graduates can expect to earn much more than non-graduates.

Your Relationship with Your Bank

Your bank is a business like any other. It is best to form a business-like relationship with it from day one.

Rule 1. Communicate. However bad things are they will only get worse if you do not talk with your bank. Discuss with them the best options for borrowing and managing your accounts. The people you talk to will probably have children of their own with the same issues and are likely to be sympathetic.

Rule 2. Choose your bank for practical reasons not because you like the freebies. You are more likely to change your partner than your bank so choose wisely. The issues to consider are:

- Do they provide easy access to cash points?

- Can I talk easily to a human being and do they have a student adviser?

- What overdraft will they give me and what are the repayment terms?

- What are their charges if I exceed my borrowing limit?

- Do they provide graduate loans and what interest do they charge?

Finally, shop around. There are substantive differences between the different banks' offerings.

Set up three different accounts with your bank:

1. **A current account.** Only keep enough in here to meet your monthly cash needs and to act as a conduit to your other accounts.

2. **A bills account.** When you do your budget, transfer enough each month into this account so that when a bill comes in you always have enough money to pay for it.

3. **A deposit account.** This is the account your student loan, your earnings, presents, and other amounts go into to keep them safe from the twin ravages of alcohol and a cash card! There is many a student, or even a graduate, who has used up all their cash under the influence of alcohol. It is not unusual for a student to have spent their entire student loan in the first week at university!

Credit

Easy credit is a modern evil or a blessing – depending upon your point of view. Lending to someone who has not thought through how they will repay the money and the consequences of that should be a crime. It is not, because we are all deemed to be responsible adults capable of making our own choices. Mmmm...

Step 1. Do I really need what I am planning to buy? In a time when house prices always rose ahead of inflation, it made more sense to spend money on a mortgage rather than paying rent. That is not true today. At the time of writing, interest rates have been at historic low levels for some years but they will not remain so for ever. Buying a house is a long-term investment and you are unlikely to pay off the mortgage through house price inflation.

A simplistic calculation

1. Borrow £200,000 at 4% = £8,000 per annum

Repayment: £200,000 divided by 25 years = £8,000 per annum

Total cost in year one – £16,000 or £1,333 per month

2. Borrow £200,000 at 8% (the average cost of borrowing in the last 20 years) = £16,000

Repayment: £8,000

Total cost £24,000(an increase of 50%) or £2,000 per month

If you are on a secure career track with an ever-rising salary then this may not be a problem. If, on the other hand, you are a nurse or teacher where your earnings are only going to grow slowly then it definitely will be.

Solution

Budget for £2,000 per month and use the extra money initially to pay down your mortgage more quickly. If you can't afford £2,000 per month then stick to renting and build up your savings or take out a smaller mortgage.

CUT UP YOUR CREDIT CARDS

Spending money on a credit card just doesn't feel like spending! Credit cards charge a substantially higher rate of interest than a bank loan (17% versus 8%) and it will take you much longer to pay it off (store cards are even more expensive). It is easy to get into a credit card spiral where you use one card to pay off another and the debt just continues to grow. It is much better to have a charge card where you pay off the total each month. Above all – think before you buy. Do I really, really need this. Can I afford it?

The Three Big Savers

There are two and possibly three major items you will want to save for during your lifetime. Buying a house we have discussed and the other two are saving for school fees and a pension.

Pensions

Most people do not start worrying about a pension until it is too late. To provide an income of £30,000 in retirement you need a pension pot of £600,000. To save £600,000 over 40 years you need to save £15,000 a year, including investment growth. If you try and do it in 20 years you obviously need to save £30,000 a year – an impossibility for most people – and you are unlikely to be rescued by trading down your house as the previous generation have done. So, start saving as much as you can afford, as early as possible. There are going to be a lot of people in poverty in their old age in the years ahead.

A mortgage

I have covered this above but it makes it even more important to consider this rationally in the light of school fees and a pension. You need to think hard about your priorities and plan.

Insurance

Insurance is there to protect against catastrophic loss, e.g. a loss you cannot afford. Whenever you insure, ask yourself "If I didn't insure this and something happened, what would be the result?" Let us look at some examples:

- **Life insurance.** If I were to die and my income was lost to my family how would they cope? If you are a single person without any debt the answer is probably fine! If you are the main earner in your family and your salary is funding the mortgage, school fees, and the majority of the living costs then the result would be catastrophic.

- **Group Income Protection.** This is insurance that pays out a substantial proportion of your salary if you become ill and cannot work. If you have significant monthly commitments this could be very important.

- **House insurance.** if your house were to burn down where would you live and how would you afford it? Only the very, very stupid would consider not insuring their house but you might take a view on the contents. It usually costs around £70,000 to furnish a house from start to finish but you could do it for less or accept an orange box lifestyle for a while.

- **Private medical insurance.** A luxury you might think, but as the pressure on the health service grows it may start restricting availability. Free on the point of delivery may become impossible for a future government and health delivery may be means tested. If you have mental health problems, private care is the only viable option.

- **Car insurance.** A legal necessity but if you have an old banger do you need fully comprehensive? It makes much more sense to buy a cheap older car and run it into the ground rather than buy a shiny new one that depreciates by 60% in three years. You could also ask yourself – do I need a car at all?

An alternative to insurance, if the result of a loss is not catastrophic, is to self-insure – you put aside a certain amount each month rather than paying the money to an insurance company. Many large companies self-insure their risk exposure.

Conclusion

It will be apparent that the key to a happy and prosperous life is to plan and to budget. Life is too financially complicated today to leave it to chance. Review your budget every six months and adjust accordingly. Above all, accept that unless you are very rich, you cannot have it all and choices will have to be made.

CASE STUDY

The principal skill to be utilised in relation to your campaign is budgeting and your sixth form budget might look like this:

		Notes
Number of pupils now	87	(a)
Fee	£18,000 per annum	(b)
Gross income	£1,566,000	(c) = (a) x (b)
Discounts/bursaries	£156,000	(d)
Net income	£1,410,000	(c) - (d)
Expenses per annum		
Staff costs	£1,335,000	Include employers N.I and pension costs.

Other costs	£225,000	
Total	£1,560,000	Assumes no major building or other capital costs. These would be written off over a number of years and be shown in your budget as depreciation
Loss	£150,000	
Break-even (no of pupils)	97	£1,560,000/£16,200 (net fee after discounts etc)

So your first objective must be to add ten pupils to get to break even. In addition you might want to show a cash flow as the money to be spent on refurbishing the centre would be spent before any fee income had been received.

Item	July	Aug	Sept
Opening balance	0	-£200,000	-£200,000
Cash in	0	0	£523,800 (97 x £5,400)
Cash out	£200,000		£111,250 (salaries)
Closing balance	-£200,000	-£200,000	£212,550

In practice, your cash flow would extend over the full year or even beyond so that you can see when you might expect the money back from your £200,000 refurbishment cost of the sixth form centre. For example, if you have 100 pupils, your profit (contribution) is the income from three pupils or £48,600 so it would take over four years to recoup the £200,000 investment. You would hope to do better than that.

Chapter Summary

I hope you recognise the importance of good financial sense and of planning and budgeting. It is never too early to start developing good habits with money and these will serve you very well throughout your life. If you have never done a spread sheet, you should learn how to do so as this form of budgeting is very useful and recognised the world over. Good luck with managing your money!

In the next chapter, we move on to interview skills and career planning.

Further Reading

Cut the Cost of Uni, Gwenda Thomas (Trotman, 2012)

Educational Grants Directory, Alan French and Tom Traynor, (Directory of Social Change)

The Grants Register (Palgrave Macmillan)

The Charities Digest (Waterlow Information Services)

CHAPTER EIGHT
Interviewing Skills and Career Planning

Chapter Overview

"So tell me what you want, what you really, really, want…" This did very well as an anthem for the Spice Girls and in terms of your career planning you could use it as your personal anthem. It's so important that you know what you want and that you have a plan to achieve your goals. In order to realise your goals and get the life and career that you really, really want, you will most likely have to undergo many interviews – for both those coveted university places and the jobs for which you will apply through your working life. As you probably know, it's a highly competitive world out there. Unless you prepare well for your interviews and have firm career goals in mind, you won't get very far. This chapter will help you shine in interviews and will also provide a useful guide for career planning.

Simon Cowell probably wouldn't have gone for "So tell me what you want, well, sort of, on a good day"!

Developing Brilliant Interview Skills

If you follow this four-step process I can assure you that you will shine at every interview you attend.

- **STEP ONE:** Prepare well

- **STEP TWO:** Make a good first impression

- **STEP THREE:** Use excellent communication skills by asking good questions and answering interview questions clearly and succinctly

- **STEP FOUR:** Make a good final impression

Let's look at these individually.

Step One: Preparing for the Interview

Like just about everything in life, preparation is very important. Give yourself plenty of time to prepare for each and every interview. Here are some of the things you should do:

- Research the organisation to which you are applying. Look at their web site; find out what the media and press have been saying about them; research the position you are applying for

- Make sure you do the same for any university or higher education institution to which you are applying

- Anticipate questions you might be asked and develop answers for them

- Prepare questions to ask the interviewer/s

- Consider how you will get to the interview – build in a margin of error on timing just in case there are transport problems or other delays

- Plan your interview outfit. Dress appropriately: comfortable shoes, jacket, suit or skirt. Minimise jewellery and, for both genders, remember this motto: "More flesh – less authority" so cover up chest, shoulders and thighs.

- Consider your strengths and what you can bring to the organisation. Be prepared to talk about your strengths and give examples. One way to do this is to use the STAR system. STAR stands for Situation – Task – Action – Result. Try this exercise. Choose three of your personal strengths from the list below. Feel free to add other strengths that you feel are relevant to you.
  - Planning
  - Oral communication
  - Written communication
  - Influencing
  - Organisational
  - Presentation
  - Analytical
  - People
  - Teamwork
  - Leadership
  - Problem solving/lateral thinking
  - Numeracy
  - Decision-making
  - IT
  - Creative ability
  - Resourcefulness
  - Prioritising
  - Common sense

- Tenacity

- Technical skills

- Drive

- Big picture thinking

- Project management

- Meeting deadlines

- Decision-making.

For each strength, think of at least one story you can tell that will illustrate how you demonstrated that strength or skill. Describe the situation, talk about the task you faced, then the action you took and the result achieved. This is a very effective way of communicating your skills and, again, I strongly advise you to prepare these examples in advance.

STAR example: Let's imagine that one of your skills is good written communication and you have been asked in an interview to demonstrate how you have used this skill.

Situation: Your sixth form head student team decided to develop a termly newsletter to be sent to parents, staff and governors.

Task: You were asked to take on the editorship of the newsletter working with a small team of writers, designers and photographers.

Action: You developed a timetable, allocated activities and determined which articles needed to be written and what the theme of the first newsletter would be. You then wrote the front page article and the editorial opinion piece.

Result: The first newsletter was published and distributed on time and was widely praised by staff and parents. You were editor for a year and produced three issues.

Actually, this example not only demonstrates your written skills, but also leadership, team working and organisational capabilities. Of course, you will have kept copies of the newsletter!

Step Two: Making a Great Impression

In the next chapter you will read about making a good impression on others. I urge you to read this chapter very well. The advice given will help you make positive impacts in every interview you undergo. Let's consider how you make positive impressions:

- Arrive on time and be well prepared

- Look professional in your dress and deportment

- Enter the room with confidence – back straight, shoulders back, good eye contact and remember to smile – it makes you look as if you are pleased to be there

- If the interviewer offers to shake your hand, respond with a firm handshake and look the person in the eye for as long as it takes you to identify the colour of their irises – so about three to five seconds

- Sit when invited to do so

- Don't slouch in the chair but keep your back straight

- When you are answering questions, lean forward towards to person you are addressing – this demonstrates interest and enthusiasm

- Actively listen to others

- Take notes

Step Three: Managing the Interview with Excellent Communication

The purpose of any interview is to find out as much as possible about you and to test your knowledge and your suitability for the position. The questions you ask indicate several things to the interviewer or interviewing panel:

- How seriously you are thinking about the position and how well you understand what the chosen subject or job is about

- What is important to you and what your expectations are

- How much research you did on the university or organisation

- Your degree of common sense and intellectual curiosity

- Your energy level and communication skills

- Your level of maturity

Topics for your own questions:

One way to build good questions is to identify a core set of topics about which you can speak. This makes the task of asking questions easier while also focusing your questions on subjects important to your interviewer. Four topics are especially useful:

1. The degree course or job

2. The university or company

3. The department/faculty or team you will be working with

4. Your interests and experience

5. Why you feel you are suited to the course or the position

Written questions:

Should you write some of your questions in advance and bring them to the interview?

- Yes, by all means – it will help you articulate your thoughts. Bring them to the interview in a notebook or on 3x5 cards. If you want to refer to them, say: "I have written down a number of questions. Would you mind if I refer to my notes?" Don't read your questions verbatim. Glance at your notes to jog your memory and maintain good eye contact when you ask them.

These are some of the questions you should be prepared to answer:

- What attracted you to apply to this university/college/department/course?

- What do you think you can contribute to this position?

- Would you consider yourself a team player? Why?

- What are your strengths?

- What would you consider to be your weaknesses?

- How do you respond to pressure and deadlines?

- What particular areas of your subject do you like best?

- Do you have an idea of what you would like to do with your degree when you qualify?

- What are your interests outside school?

Topics for your own questions:

- If I'm the successful candidate, what would success look like in one year's time?

- What do you think are the best things about working for this organisation?

- Can you give me the feel of a typical week/month, and some of the things I'll be expected to do on a regular basis?

- What are the opportunities for growth in this position?

- May I ask what attracted you to join this organisation?

And finally…some really awful questions that you should never ask in a job interview!

- What does your company do?

- Are you (the interviewer) married?

- I'm not really a morning person. Do I really have to get here by 8.30 am?

- When can I take time off? How much time do I get off?

- How long is this interview going to take?

- If I don't like my boss here, what can I do to change that?

- What is your/my boss' star sign?

- How many sick days do I get a month?

- Will I ever have to work over a weekend?

- Will I have to meet a lot of deadlines?

- When will I be promoted?

Step Four: Final Impressions

Final impressions are almost as important as first. Do make sure to do the following at the end of the interview:

- Thank the interviewer for his/her time

- Ask about next steps

- Shake hands (if appropriate)

- Reiterate how keen you are to join the university/organisation

- Ask if they need any further information from you

- Leave the room as you entered with confidence and positive body language

Career Planning

Let's now turn our attention to career planning and setting career goals. Before you shout, "But I don't know yet what I want to do", please understand that I am not suggesting you should know without a doubt what you want to do, but it is still helpful to set some goals and to consider your values, skills, abilities and work preferences.

This section will help you:

- Get clarity about what you actually want

- Understand what you have to offer

- Be clear about the steps you need to take

- Create a plan for the way forward

- Discover a goal-setting method that you can use throughout your life

So, with that in mind, we are going to go through a series of exercises which will help you focus your thoughts on three things:

- What is important to you

- How you see your future

- What you can do to get the future you want

You can and should use these techniques at any time in your life. Remember there are no wrong answers here – it's your life.

What's most important to me in my life?

- Consider what's important to you in your life. You can use the list below to focus your thoughts. Identify at least five values that are important to you.
    - Power
    - Security
    - Success
    - Adventure
    - Humour
    - Love
    - Independence
    - Personal growth
    - Making a difference
    - Physical appearance
    - Joy

- Personal expression

- Comfort

- Spirituality

- Caring for others

- Friendship

Feel free to add to this list.

- Now consider what's important to you in an organisation you work for. This might include many of the values you listed above. Again, feel free to add to them.

- Next, identify what's most important to you in a boss you report to. Take a look at the list below and add as you wish:

  - Fairness

  - Fun

  - Directed

  - Role model

  - Integrity

  - Good leader

  - Team player

  - Independence

  - Authority

  - Tenacity

  - Good coach

  - Punctual

  - Friendly

  - Respected

- Experienced manager

- Good communicator

• Finally, identify three people whose jobs really interest you. Carefully consider what it is about their jobs that you find interesting.

Now we move on to the most important activity – setting your **Personal Career Vision and Action Plan**. I'd like you to give some careful thought to the questions below:

• What do I hope to be doing in five years' time?

_____
_____
_____
_____
_____

• What skills will I be using? (Refer back to the list you made earlier on in this chapter)

_____
_____
_____
_____
_____

- What skills should I be developing for the future?

_____
_____
_____
_____
_____

- What type of organisation do I want to be working for?

_____
_____
_____
_____
_____

- Where will I be located?

_____
_____
_____
_____
_____

- What will I be enjoying about my life and work?

_____
_____
_____

_____

_____

- Objectives over next year (see below)

✎

_____

_____

_____

_____

_____

Now choose five objectives from the following checklist and write them into your Career Action Plan.

- 'Shadow' someone working in a career field I am exploring

- Contact any alumni of my school who are working in a professional area of interest to me

- Visit schools, colleges and establishments offering education or training in the career field I have identified

- Take a course in my area of interest

- Read a book about my area of interest

- Do volunteer work in my area of interest

- Get a part-time job in my area of interest

- Arrange a careers guidance interview

- Use the web and careers library to research areas of interest

- Ask people I meet about their careers and career paths

- Interview people who work in career areas of interest

- Prepare a basic Curriculum Vitae (CV) and adjust it for any work I apply for

- Consider doing voluntary work

- Complete a work experience or work placement opportunity to add to my skills

- Attend career fairs

- Discuss my personal statement for my UCAS form in line with my values, skills and preferences with an adviser

- Research companies/industries I have an interest in and find out if they have 'information days' or further information they can direct me towards

- Shortlist and find out more about specific jobs, careers, employers or gap year or year-out opportunities

- Prepare a covering letter to go with my CV

- Start keeping a record of all careers I have an interest in

- Take responsibility for getting the sort of grades and experience an employer will value

- Work out what skills I need to develop

- Join an association or club related to my career goals

Again, I want to emphasise that your career vision and action plan does not need to be cast in concrete – quite the opposite. It should be updated at least once a year and will change as you yourself grow and your life takes you in different directions. What's important here is to have some sense of direction in your

life and career and writing this down helps you focus and gives
goals to work towards.

Your CV

There are plenty of guides on the web on how to write effective
CVs and personal statements – just Google if you haven't
already done so. There are also a great many books on interviewing, writing CVs and career planning. Check the biblio-
graphy at the end of this chapter. You might also take a look at
www.monster.co.uk for some excellent advice and examples.
You should also speak to your careers adviser at school as well
as your head of sixth form. They will certainly have examples
they can share as well as advice to give you.

Following is an outline you might want to follow when preparing your CV. Try to keep it succinct – no more than two pages
maximum.

Curriculum Vitae

NAME:

ADDRESS:

TELEPHONE:

E-MAIL:

DATE OF BIRTH:

SCHOOLS ATTENDED:

GCSEs TAKEN:

AS SUBJECTS:

A-LEVEL SUBJECTS:

SCHOOL ACTIVITIES:

SPORTS AND HOBBIES:

ACHIEVEMENTS:

WORK EXPERIENCE:

Your CV should be sent with a succinct covering letter. Here are some tips from Monster.co.uk:

Covering Letter Tips for New Graduates

The employment outlook for new graduates is still gloomy, but you have a good chance of landing a job if you launch an aggressive search. A well-crafted covering letter should be part of this proactive strategy – experts say that customising your letter can open doors to new opportunities. Here's how.

Know the employer

While distributing the same covering letter to every employer saves time, you won't stand out from the crowd of applicants doing the same thing. You need to go online and try and find out as much as possible about the company in question and what their business is looking for. Going the extra mile not only shows your willingness to make an effort but will also help you realise if this company would be a good fit for you on a personal level.

What to include

You might lack real-world work experience, but your covering letter can be chock-full of activities that demonstrate your potential to succeed.

These activities could include volunteer work, class projects and extra-curricular activities, as well as special interest projects such as travelling, reading and music.

When it comes to being a new graduate, you may wish to take advantage of any high/stand-out academic achievements. If you took initiative in any school activities that show leadership or qualities around being a team player, these are worth mentioning. Anyone can write about being a 'great team player' but it's your real life examples that will help the recruiter understand how you will demonstrate these skills in the workplace.

Covering letter format

Your covering letter is not your autobiography – hit on the key points that would interest employers, but keep the letter short.

Include a brief opening paragraph that mentions the specifics of the position you are targeting, followed by four to five bullets reflecting qualifications that are relevant to their requirements.

The final paragraph should end with a bang – clearly state how you would contribute to the employer's operation, and confidently ask for an interview.

Unsure of your career goal?

Do some career exploration before writing a covering letter. Hiring managers should not have to figure out how your skills meet their needs. Do that work for them. If you have more than one possible direction, write different covering letters for each objective.

As you gain clarity about what you're good at and most want, you'll be ready to communicate from a genuine, confident place.

And an example of a covering letter:

Dear [INSERT HIRING MANAGER'S NAME],

Regarding the [INSERT JOB TITLE] position currently advertised on Monster.co.uk, please find attached a copy of my CV for your consideration.

I have recently graduated with a [INSERT GRADE] in [INSERT SUBJECT] from [INSERT UNIVERSITY] and hope to put this to use in the field of [INSERT INDUSTRY SECTOR].

The course covered many topics, and I was particularly drawn to [INSERT SPECIFIC TOPIC]. I am looking to develop specialist skills in this area and build a successful career.

INCLUDE IF YOU HAVE UNDERTAKEN WORK EXPERIENCE

I have put my course theory into practice in a variety of ways, most effectively as a [INSERT JOB TITLE] at [INSERT COMPANY NAME] where I [INSERT KEY ACHIEVEMENT].

Having extensively researched your company's values and products, I was especially interested in [INSERT COMPANY ASPECT THAT ATTRACTED YOU].I feel it would be the ideal place for me to begin my career and I believe I can be an excellent addition to your team.

If you would like to get in touch to discuss my application and to arrange an interview, you can contact me via [INSERT PHONE NUMBER OR E-MAIL ADDRESS].

I look forward to hearing from you soon.

Yours sincerely

[INSERT NAME]

These examples are for graduates, but you are not far off and the principles remain the same.

The top ten tips for successful career planning

- Be clear on your values, skills and preferences
- Research career options and opportunities
- Network – take another look at Chapter 3
- Increase your employment skills through shadowing and work experience
- Write a really good CV and covering letter
- Set yourself clear goals
- Get the best qualifications you can
- Keep a portfolio of your work experience and achievements
- Work on your career vision – update it at least once a year
- Prepare well before every interview

CASE STUDY

You should document the work you do on the campaign so you can use it as an example of your strengths and skills. This is just the sort of thing that future employers will be impressed by. Keep a copy of the campaign plan and any reports or presentations you develop. Keep photographs, event materials, invitations etc. These can be combined into a portfolio which you can show at interviews (when appropriate) and refer to in years to come.

It would be excellent if you could get your head teacher or a member of the board of governors to write a short testimonial on you and the work you have done. This is as good as a positive job reference.

Of course, this is a fictional case study but the principles remain the same. Do keep records of any special programmes you work on or impressive extra-curricular activities you engage with. Having a portfolio demonstrating your skills and experience is extremely valuable and well worth the time to put it together.

Chapter Summary

In this chapter we have looked at the four-step process for doing brilliant interviews and suggested some questions you might ask in an interview as well as questions the interviewer might well ask you. We have also looked at career planning and identifying your career vision and you have had the opportunity to think about your goals, particularly where you want to be in five years' time. Finally, we have looked at writing a CV and covering letter and provided some useful tips on both. The rest is up to you and the authors wish you every success as you embark on your life beyond school.

Next we turn to the chapter on personal branding and making an impact – highly relevant in terms of what we have just been discussing.

Further Reading

Successful Interview Skills: How to Prepare, Answer Tough Questions and Get Your Ideal Job, Rebecca Corfield (Kogan Page, 2009)

The Graduate Career Guidebook: Advice for Students and Graduates on Careers Options, Jobs, Volunteering, Applications..., Steve Rook (Palgrave Macmillan, 2013)

Brilliant Interview, Ros Jay (Brilliant Business, Prentice Hall, 2010)

Brilliant Career Coach: How to Find and Follow Your Dream Career, Sophie Rowan (Brilliant Business, Pearson, 2011)

Goal Setting Workbook: How to Set Goals and Objectives Effectively to Achieve Personal Goals, Mike C. Adams (Kindle edition)

Setting Goals Worksheet with 7 Goal Setting Templates!, Paul Maxwell (Create Spaces Independent Publishing Platform)

Setting Goals (Harvard Pocket Mentor Series) Harvard Business School Press

www.monster.co.uk

CHAPTER NINE
Personal Branding: Making an Impact

By DR CRISTINA SAMBROOK

Chapter Overview

Like any brand that sells well, Brand YOU needs extensive background work and maintenance.

In this chapter, we look at how best to discover yourself, your values, accept who you are and then promote your brand in the most effective way possible. We explore how people's first impressions of you create an unconscious ready-made image that is hard to dispel, and how you can take advantage of those first impressions by having the ABCs of **Executive Presence** – the right **Appearance, Behaviour** and **Communication** to promote your brand and secure your goals.

When you walk through the door, it is **you** who wins or loses the business, interview or whatever is at stake. **You** are your own best business card. This chapter covers succinctly how best to construct and present Brand YOU.

Personal Branding – 'Know Thyself'

In a world where fame and money are the alphas and omegas of success, having a 'personal brand' has become an essential ingredient for achieving success. We are all bombarded with images of celebrities enjoying their temporary fame. Kids these days want to grow up and 'be famous' rather than having the traditional job that, only a few generations ago, would have been cherished. We are exposed to brands that trigger our imagination and desires – we want what they have, we want to be known, we want to get 'up there'.

We are not going to analyse the somewhat superficial world of celebrities. Instead, we want to look into what makes a personal brand stand out and how you can use that to your advantage, whether you are applying for a job, building a career or just representing yourself in society. The earlier you start building your personal brand, the more chances you have of developing a strong presence, with high impact, gravitas and power to influence.

David Ogilvy, the 'Father of Advertising', defined a brand as *"a intangible sum of a product's attributes, its name, packaging and price, its history, reputation, and the way it's advertised. A brand is also defined by a consumer's impression of people who use it, as well as their own experience."* In other words, it's not only what you are, who you are and what you stand for but also, and most importantly, how others perceive you, their impression of you – whether it's objective or biased by their own personal experiences.

In marketing theory – and personal branding is about marketing yourself and your brand – there are at least two important concepts that we will cover: brand identity and brand image. Identity is the first part of Ogilvy's definition: who you are, how you define your values and history, and how you project yourself to others. The image is what they think of you, how you are viewed.

A strong brand has no gap between what it wants to project and what others 'get' when seeing it; the message sent is the same as the message received (and of course, we assume it is the right one!).

Question: Where should you start in building your own brand, and how can you make it a strong one?

Having dealt with generations of hard-working students, eager to build a successful career and willing to invest time and money in either studying more, or getting internships and jobs, the author was surprised to find out how little time they dedicate to self-exploration and career planning. We are not talking here about listing your skills ahead of a job interview, but what you actually believe in and stand for – **defining Brand YOU.**

The best way to sell a brand is highlighting its competitive advantage – what makes it more attractive/desirable than its competitors, or stand out in consumers' eyes as the only appropriate choice?

You can find your 'competitive advantage' through objective, honest self-exploration that should include:

- Defining your **values.** What is most important to you? (Think who influences you in defining this, and if it's ultimately the right influence)

- Listing your **aptitudes.** What is it that you do well and enjoy doing; or maybe something that you're very good at but can still be further developed?

- What is your **personality** – extrovert / introvert, independent/dependent, light/ serious, impetuous/wary etc? (Be honest, include aspects you find hard to accept!)

- What are your **attitudes/beliefs?** Do you feel strongly about something (work or personal) if you believe something to be true and you accept it

- What are your **drivers** – what motivates you, what do you want to finally achieve? Is it money, fame, power, respect, caring for others, helping to solve problems, something else? Think about your dream job and why you want it – what comes with it that you couldn't do without?

- What **makes you happy?** What does happiness means to you (if different from previous answer)?

- What are you **willing to sacrifice** in order to get and keep your dream job? (Time, money, socialising etc.)

- What are your **achievements and skills?**

- Your opinion of your **appearance** (grooming, clothes, appropriateness for what you want your next career step to be... and beyond)

- What is it that you **need to develop/improve/change?**

- What makes you **unique** (personally and professionally)?

- What makes you **interesting?** ... We get blank stares almost every time we ask students (or clients) this – most are convinced they are not interesting. Nothing could be further from the truth! Think about what you could tell a complete stranger about you that would make him/her remember the encounter. Do you speak any foreign languages? Do you have interesting talents, hobbies, interests? Did something happen to you that is unusual (and we don't mean being kidnapped by UFOs – although of course if that did happen it might be worth a mention...)? Are your personal circumstances different?

Once you have answers to all the items in the 'know-thyself' list, read them again and underline in red all those elements that carry negative connotations. Ask yourself:

- Are they really problematic aspects?

- Are they justified (or have you blown up something out of proportion and you are generalising based on one incident)?

- Do others think the same of you?

Perception Assessment

Once you have identified your strengths and weaknesses it's worth doing a little exercise called **Perception Assessment** that involves the following steps:

1. Write a list of between five and seven words or phrases that best describe your self-perception. Those words describe your brand – that's your brand identity!

2. Write a second list of between five and seven words or phrases that describe how you think others perceive you in general.

3. You have probably heard of 360-degree feedback – in management speak it means getting others' views of you and your performance. Individuals at all levels score you on certain competences, skills and your interactions with them etc.

Perception Assessment is similar, but more in-depth about you as a person, not just for work/school purposes. It's an extremely efficient way of getting feedback on you from teachers, friends, mentors and people that you know and respect. Get them to score the two lists on their level of agreement/disagreement (from one to five) and the advice they would offer you in order to improve or increase your presence and impact, the strength of your **brand.**

Also, ask them about your voice, your smile, eye contact, facial expressions, general demeanour, posture, walk, handshake and your appearance, i.e. grooming and clothes.

Record the answers on an 'on-going action list' so that you can refer to them from time to time as you work through the **Image Ingredients:**

- Voice

- Facial expression

- Demeanour

- Posture

- Walk

- Handshake

- Smile

- Eye contact

- Grooming and clothes

You will then get a clearer image of how people actually perceive you and what you need to improve (if anything).

Your Goal

Once you have details from the self-discovery exercise, as well as the report on how people that matter perceive you, bear in mind that this is your current image with (maybe) some suggestions on potential development.

However, your personal goals should start having an impact on how you shape your identity. Developing your personal brand should start as early in your career as possible.

Your personal development plan starts with the questions: "Where do I see myself in five years from now?" "What is my career going to look like?" "What is my dream job?" You may remember that we covered these sorts of questions in the previous chapter and they are particularly relevant here as well.

Exercise

The casting director

Here is a very useful little exercise – repeat it every so often, as you progress through your career:

Imagine you are the casting director of a multi-million dollar movie. You can afford to cast any A-list Hollywood actor/actress you want in the role of a successful ____(fill in with your dream job)___

Now think about what 'appearance' traits they should have. Of course we are playing with stereotypes, but it's advisable to do this as objectively as you can. Write down a list about:

What clothes should they wear?

_____

_____

_____

_____

_____

How should they do their hair? (up/down for women, short/modern/classic etc. for men)

_____

_____

_____

_____

_____

How should they walk (if posture matters...)? What shoes should they wear?

_____

_____

_____

_____

_____

What level of grooming should they have?

✐

_____

_____

_____

_____

_____

What is their body language (eye contact, posture, facial expressions, demeanour)?

✐

_____

_____

_____

_____

_____

How should they communicate? How confident should they be? (How would you tell if they are confident or not?)?

✐

_____

_____

_____

_____

_____

What is the Difference Between That Image and YOU?

Confidence and strong impact come from self-acceptance.

Accept yourself warts 'n' all! – all your physicals traits, quirks and personal characteristics.

You should always have, and convey, a strongly defined sense of self so that others receive that message about you too.

It may be expedient however, with certain people or in certain situations, to either conceal some particular aspects of yourself or highlight others – you are after all selling your competitive advantage and pointing out the positives! This doesn't change who you are and doesn't mean that you compromise yourself – it certainly doesn't mean you are not authentic. Think of how you choose to dress differently for different occasions, e.g. a wedding or going to the gym: you still are the same person, merely accommodating people and the situation appropriately.

It's just clever packaging of your brand!

Elevator Pitch

Using the knowledge of personal traits described so far, the content of your personal introduction should create enough interest in others that they remember you and want to get to know you better.

Imagine getting in an elevator: ground floor, you press the top floor button; doors are about to close when someone pushes in and presses the top floor button too. He/she could be one of the most important people in your life – the one that gets you your first important job. You have 60 seconds (to the top floor) to make a good impression on them, and interest them enough to give you their business card. What would you say?

Your **'elevator pitch'** is a quick and concise way to communicate who you are, what you do, and why you do it better or differently... and subtly how it may interest or benefit them. It's your 'pitch'.

Create a variety of different templates giving significant facts that would be relevant to different respondents and situations – and that would make them want to know more.

They all should include your name, who you are, what you do, and something that differentiates you from others seemingly doing the same thing. Some should contain a little lightness/humour but all should be short (between fifteen seconds and three minutes) and to the point.

You need to consider carefully all the reasons they could and should be interested in you and/or what you do, and the selection of pitches should be created with that in mind.

Your aim is to engage the listener and possibly to stimulate them to take any action that puts them on a path to do what it is you want. At the very least, to want to hear more!

First Impressions

So you had your elevator encounter with the imaginary CEO that could give you a job: what do you think they thought of you? What kind of impressions did they get of you?

When someone encounters you for the first time, they will make a considerable number of assumptions about you of which they may not even be conscious.

Some 'facts' may be proven wrong in time – like your education, type of work, status, background, etc. However, they undoubtedly will have also drawn other conclusions about you – your personality, attitude, level of empathy, etc. They form an opinion about you based on your appearance, how you are

dressed, your body language, your demeanour, your manner-
isms and this is how they will think of you – and describe you to
others.

It is their perception of you – the impression you have made on
them.

Research proves a whole range of assumptions are instantly
made; you have probably heard phrases like 'you only get one
chance to make a first impression'. These assumptions become
conclusions as they are unquestioned and become the owner's
reality. They create a filter from thereon in through which you
will continue to be perceived. Unlikely to be revisited, that perception is rarely changed... unless it is made to be.

Exercise

A commuter special, any line to any destination

Any day, any month...

> *You are sitting on a packed commuter train reading an
> interesting book. The woman opposite you answers
> her mobile but irritates you with the conversation; you
> can't focus on your story and are forced to listen to
> what she's saying.*

> *As you near your destination, you both stand up and
> collide. Her bag drops and the contents spill out. You
> help her to pick them up then walk together towards
> the exit, making small talk.*

A week later...

You hear the TV news in the background: an unidentified body of a woman has been found some 60 miles away and the police are asking for help. A photo is flashed up (found in her pocket) and you recognise the young woman as the one from your train, last week.

You pick up the phone to call the police... You may not think you can help, but you feel you have to let them know you had met her, albeit briefly.

You certainly made some judgements at the time – consciously or subconsciously, some stronger than others. They might have included age, ethnicity, background, social status, class, health/fitness, wealth, mood, family/marital status, lifestyle, education, type of work, cleanliness, lifestyle, intelligence, personality, aptitude – nerdy, athletic, arty etc.

Write down how you made those judgements, assumptions – what would you be looking at?

The same areas of 'assumptions' will be valid for you too. Others will look at these criteria and judge you!

Combine the results from this exercise with the ones from **The casting director** – you now have an extensive list of areas where people will form an image of you. Make sure it's the right image!

Whether it is to start or advance your career or improve your social life, it's important to know how to create a **good** first impression.

Situations when people make first impressions

There are only a few situations in which all first impressions take place, whether in person, or not (via phone, e-mail).

The invisible image – first impressions though e-mail

When somebody 'meets' you for the first time by e-mail they will make a first impression of you purely from your writing style – i.e. the choice of words and the way they are put together.

E-mail correspondents (particularly those whose first language is not English) may not appreciate nuance or the English sense of humour.

The need for brevity in e-mail means that it is often unqualified by the 'softening' adjectives and adverbs commonly used in English speech and in prose. This directness can sound unnecessarily harsh or critical and can cause a negative reaction. If this happens, consider carefully before making a knee-jerk response. Read out loud more 'sensitive' e-mails – if varying the tone or words you accentuate can change the final meaning (especially with negative subtext), rephrase it! When possible, use a personal salutation and exit before signing off to personalise your e-mail and to create the possibility of building a more personal relationship. Show a human side, be interesting and interested!

Telephone – another invisible image

When 'meeting' people on the telephone for the first time, they will undoubtedly leave with a first impression of you. For a positive first impression, your voice should convey:

Energy	Interest	Authority*	Professionalism
Confidence	Appropriateness	Warmth*	Conviction
Positivity	Sincerity	Humour*	Empathy

The sound of the voice is heard, absorbed and assessed before the contents. It is made up of several adjustable components that both affect the expectation and alter the meaning of the words. These components should be used together to create a voice that is pleasant sounding, varied in order to hold interest, and appropriate to the message and the situation.

The remainder of the First Impression comes from the choice of words and the way they are put together.

If you have a voicemail message, make sure it creates a good impression – it could just be the first – and last!

Meetings and Interviews

When you walk in the door, the first impression of you is made:

55% on how you look (appearance and body language)

38% on the sound of your voice

7% on what you say (content)

If you make enough positive impact with the first two, what you say will have a much more effective result. You will be more likely to be listened to, taken seriously, believed, respected and remembered. You will also find that you are more able to influence and inspire others too. You will remember that we covered this topic in Chapter 2 and it is extremely relevant to the subject of this chapter as well.

The ABCs of Your Executive Presence

The Centre for Talent Innovation (CTI), a heavyweight US think-tank, recently published a report concluding, with management competence being a given, that Executive Presence ('being perceived as leadership material')is undoubtedly the essential ingredient needed to get to the top of organisations. "How you look, how you speak, and how you act turn out to be critical to your success *[the report concludes],* at every step in your career journey."

The ABCs (Appearance, Behaviour and Communication) of Executive Presence have therefore a long-lasting impact on your success.

[A]: Your Appearance:

Survey your clothes: are they appropriate for the message you want to send out? Will people think of you as accomplished, successful and the right ambassador for your organisation /school/university/family? Do you represent 'excellence'? (This applies to all interactions you have – whether for a job interview, important meeting or normal social interactions.)

- It is important that your clothes are appropriate and 'feel right' for the situation – the right cut, shape, items make you look good and feel good. You are comfortable and not constrained, which shows positively in your body language; you feel confident and able to portray yourself in the most flattering of lights!

- Start building a wardrobe that works for you. Fit, co-ordinate, accessorise appropriately. Express your personality, but don't be extreme in dressing. Be aware of fashion, but not its slave. If you want to stand out from the crowd, stand out for the right reason – as well dressed, groomed and with a positive image!

Complete the picture with **top-to-toe grooming:** overall, this should give an impression of cleanliness and impeccability.

- People make assumptions based on it: it says to them that you respect yourself (and others!), that you care enough to communicate it with your appearance, that you pay attention to detail and aim for the best possible outcome.

- Being well groomed includes caring for your nails and hands, having well-cut and tidy hair, taking care of your skin (for women this means wearing appropriate make-up – natural, not eccentric and extreme; it should enhance and complement your features, not 'scream' at people!), good smell/hygiene, appropriate glasses/lenses, and clean teeth.

[B] Your Behaviour makes a difference!

Face and body language say more to people than they realise at a conscious level. When you look and feel well about yourself, it shows in how you stand (shoulders back, tall and vertical), how grounded you are (owning your space), how you move (gesticulate with purpose, not fidgeting), how confidently you walk, how open your body language is. The non-verbal messages you send out are basic reflectors of your own confidence and self-image.

A special note on manners and etiquette: you might think they belong to a bygone era. After all, we now communicate as quickly as possible, we text, we address each other using first names – why would we need manners and etiquette? The simple answer is that they do make a difference and people actually care! The higher up you go in your career, the more these details matter.

If you are not seen to practise this code, it could certainly count against you in certain situations. It is always best to know what is viewed as right and then make an informed decision about whether to use it or not. Speaking and behaving appropriately (good manners and etiquette) can certainly do no harm as long as it is not seen to be overdone, sycophantic or old fashioned.

Your behaviour should always be congruent with the image you are choosing to portray. For example, to project an image of maturity, authority and responsibility, you can't be seen to behave like a carefree teenager: chewing gum in an interview, texting when other people are talking to you or keeping your iPod headphones on when addressing others.

[C] Your Communication

We all communicate ideas and intentions not only through words, but our voices too! This doesn't mean one's accent, but the actual voice, pitch, speed, tone, inflexion, and timing. A high-pitched squeaky voice indicates a nervous, flibbertigibbet kind of person that lacks confidence and presence. Someone with a slow monotone voice that doesn't change in pitch with new ideas could be perceived as lacking personality or 'oomph', boring their audience to tears!

Your voice can dispel an existing image or, equally, can endorse it. A pleasant and interesting voice makes people enjoy listening to it, trusting the speaker and remembering them positively!

CASE STUDY

So how does all the information in this chapter apply to your case study?

You are a member of an extended team that represents academic excellence, the ambassadors of high perform-ance and success! The ABCs of **your** presence have to immediately communicate that message and make it clear to your interlocutors, stakeholders and observers that this is an exclusive brand, both desired and admired.

Regarding your team: Analyse who your stakeholders are and be clear on the message you want to send to them. Do your ABCs give out the right message?

- Discuss with your team members the importance of having an appropriate 'Appearance' – decide on the best approach to create a consistent image for your team, one that blends in the strengths of all members, as well as adjusting certain discrepancies.

- Analyse each other's 'Behaviour': is it targeted and on-message? Can you advise your team members on a change of attitude? Is there any negative feedback that any of you are dealing with and, if so, how can you help each other progress?

- How effectively do you 'Communicate' individually and as a team? Observe your team members when present-ing or interacting naturally, and give them feedback on their communication style and voice. Suggest rather than dictate, allude to potential improvements rather than belittle them for faults (and always deal with sensitive issues privately, face to face!). Be kind and supportive, offer encouragement and be aware that people dwell on negatives, so don't be too critical!

Create an action plan for:

- Further personal changes or adjustments

- Team work – with ways to achieve your goals, timing/deadlines, feedback/challenge process and a system for evaluating results (in doing so, use the information from the other relevant chapters).

Putting Your Personal Action Plan Together

This should result from all the exercises included in this chapter.

Once you have completed these exercises, you should:

- Know what your own brand is – what you represent, what your values are, what you want to communicate to others

- Have accepted yourself, warts'n'all!

- Have gained confidence and belief in your own abilities

- Know that personal accomplishment follows thorough scrutiny and a desire to actually improve yourself. It's a continuous process throughout life and not just limited to career development. Good luck with building your personal brand!

Chapter Summary

In this chapter we have discussed what is meant by the term 'personal brand' and looked at the key ways to develop one that is strong and memorable. We have discussed the importance of making good first impressions and different ways to introduce yourself in an impactful way – your 'elevator pitch'. We have considered the ABCs of your Executive Presence – attitude, behaviour and communication – and reviewed how all of this is relevant to the case study which runs through the book. The subject of the next and final chapter is very interesting and covers a very important aspect of education and work – how to improve your memory skills.

Further Reading

Executive Presence Report, Sylvia Ann Hewlett et al (Centre for Talent Innovation, 2012)

Managing Your Image, Laurel Herman, (Positive Presence, 3rd edition, 2006) www.positivepresence.com

Pitch Yourself: The Most Effective CV You'll Ever Write. Stand Out and Sell Yourself, B Faustand M Faust (Prentice Hall,2nd edition, 2006)

It's the Way You Say It: Becoming Articulate, Well-Spoken and Clear, Carol A Fleming (Berrett-Koehler, 2nd edition, 2013)

Creating Personal Presence: Look, Talk, Think, and Act Like a Leader, D Booher (Bennett-Koehler, 2011)

THE SIXTH-FORM MBA

CHAPTER TEN
Memory and Revision Skills

By JOHN DALTON

Chapter Overview

Preparing and passing tests is a core part of life for any student. A common misconception amongst many students is that somehow the skills gained while preparing for courses such as GCSE or A-levels (or equivalent) are not that transferable or that useful in later life. Nothing could be further from the truth. A fundamental part of any examination is **memory** and your ability to access facts and apply concepts. In this chapter we will examine the skills that are required not just for your A-levels, but for your degree and thereafter in your career and private life.

Memory and Learning

Memory is critical to most things we do and revision and learning are all linked and dependent mostly on memory recall. **Revision,** or the act of revising, is a process that involves disciplined re-reading and assessment of notes and course material to ensure that the concepts and facts involved are understood and can be applied to new, often **unfamiliar**

situations. The latter is used by examiners as a way of evaluating a student's comprehension of a topic and usually involves the concepts, especially in science and social sciences, being placed within an unfamiliar situation or context. If the student is not fazed by the unfamiliar and gets the answer right, then they have deeply understood it.

Revision involves the **encoding of short-term memory (STM) into long-term memory (LTM)** so that concepts and facts can be accessed when required. Indeed, research by London University has demonstrated a link between student memory quality and exam outcomes.

Students often make the mistake of trying to learn a topic without properly understanding it first. For example, a student who is weak in mathematics and who takes Chemistry at A-level may try and just learn facts and ideas by rote from a chemistry textbook without fully grasping the concepts involved. Such an approach is risky because, if a question is asked that requires application of the concept, then the student is not in a position to give a proper answer to the demands of the question. This is why many students who seem perfectly able in class get mediocre or poor grades in examinations. Understanding something is not easy – it takes time, dedication and desire to master the topic.

The message at this stage is loud and clear. Before you start revising a topic, first you must have **understood its essence**, the key principles involved, the context and possible applications. Although this is generally true for all subjects, it is especially critical in subjects such as biology, chemistry, physics, psychology, geography and economics. It is also true of humanities: for example, to understand a key literature book, one must understand the core theme of the book. Equally, if trying to understand reasons for a revolution in history, one must first understand its origins and the context. As a subject, mathematics is probably in a league of its own. You need to be comfortable with logic and mathematical principles to handle A-level maths, but once concepts are understood, top grades in maths are also a question of practice. **Practice** is also central to all learning – because the more you practise in a subject and apply key principles, the more your brain secures the **neuronal connections between synapses** and the connections become stronger, thus improving thinking ability and recall. Therefore, **learning is achieved through periodic repetition, not cramming the night before!**

So the basic rule of all successful revision is to:

- Understand the concepts and principles involved first and their context, plus the interdependence with other topics

- Break down each topic into smaller discrete units of understanding, focusing on key concepts and words, phrases or dates

Knowledge Management

Once you have understood the topic you will have gained knowledge which can then be applied. Please note that awareness of a topic does not equate to understanding and **knowledge**. In business, people talk about knowledge management and the importance of converting data into information and then converting the information into knowledge. Information is essentially facts about a subject, but which lacks coherence and connectedness. Knowledge suggests that some **meaning** can be gathered by connecting elements of information together. Just as business people need to convert data and information into knowledge, so do students when learning. A student with lots of information but who cannot connect this information into some meaning has limited knowledge of their subject. This is important for learning, but in the UK, education involves a mixture of **deductive and inductive instruction and reasoning**. At its simplest, deductive reasoning requires information and then draws conclusions from it. By contrast, inductive reasoning involves constructing general propositions from specific examples.

To be successful at exams, students must understand the important distinction between deductive and inductive reasoning. Although factual recall is still very much part of examinations in the UK, less emphasis is placed on it and more emphasis on inductive reasoning, whereby the student is asked to make predictions or provide answers about a problem based on existing knowledge. If a student does not understand or have sound knowledge of the topic, then when presented with inductive reasoning problems, they cannot easily answer the question because they cannot apply their knowledge to this new situation. **This is why understanding is critical for application.**

Some of my weaker students select a chapter of a book, go home and read the chapter and claim afterwards that they have understood it. When asked some basic questions that tease out important principles, they can be hazy on details. For example, a student of mine told me that he would go home and read a chapter from two separate text books on evolution for his A-level biology revision. When he returned the next day he confidently asked me to test him – so I did. I simply asked him if individuals or populations evolve, to which he responded individuals. At this point I knew he had failed to grasp a key concept in evolutionary biology – only populations can evolve, not individuals. This student, who was very bright, had committed the classic mistake of reading and making himself aware of a topic, but failing to properly comprehend its key concepts.

The good news is that such a common mistake is easily rectified by good practice and **structured learning and revision**. Before any student attempts to improve revision and memory skills, there are some important points that must be first addressed:

1. Understand yourself and your strengths and weaknesses in terms of learning

2. Find your material

3. Organise yourself and your environment

4. Learn the subject using comprehension and memory

5. Consolidate the learning

Understand yourself. What type of person are you, how might this influence your ability and discipline to revise? What are your strengths and weaknesses? How do you best learn? What is your thinking style and approach? What motivates you to learn?

What are the main barriers to learning? Before you go any further in learning and revision, you must first address yourself and your fears. My experience tells me that fear, and not cognitive (thinking) ability is one of the greatest drawbacks to learning and progress. Students often become fatalistic and victims of their own **stereotype.** By this I mean that they begin to falsely believe in a fixed and somewhat oversimplified idea or notion about themselves, e.g. "I am no good at mathematics", or "I am poor at data questions or interpreting poetry". When I ask a class who is good at x or y, you notice hands go up without the students even having time to consider the question carefully. They immediately believe that they are good or bad at a subject. This is what I describe as a **false dichotomy** in learning – that there are only two realities, when often the truth is far more complex and hazy.

Students who believe a certain stereotype about themselves may be creating massive mental blocks to learning, without any real independent evidence for it. It may be based on a few bad experiences of the past or a few ill-chosen words from parents or teachers. If you know that maths is not your strong suit, then acknowledge the deficiency and work at it.

Do NOT avoid or mentally clam up when a question appears that involves some basic proficiency in mathematics. Most of the time, when shown the solution, you understand it.

Other terrible barriers to learning are habit and procrastination. Habits are routine behaviours that we often find difficult to give up, and indeed, may draw comfort from them. Students often have very negative or limiting habits that act as a barrier to new experience, realities and learning; for example, students who listen to music while trying to revise or always go off with friends for some fun after a revision session. Although both examples are fairly harmless in themselves, they both cause interference in **consolidating the encoding of material into long-term memory for recall.** Procrastination means failing to act and simply putting off a decision to do something. We all suffer to some extent from this, but in certain people this is a real psychological and behavioural barrier to action and progress.

Once you understand yourself better, in an honest, transparent way, then you are in a better position to correct your weaknesses and champion your strengths. The biggest barrier to effective revision is **self-deception**. So many students (and their baffled parents) claim that "Claire or John spends many hours studying in their room, so I just do not understand why they are not doing as well as they should". This is part of the self-deception game, which is visited on many of us into adult and professional life. Students often equate long hours spent in their room looking at books and reading as quality revision. Yet after four hours of such activity, they can recall or understand only a handful of concepts: why? The simple answer is that **quantity does not equate to quality**; many students who revise for long periods believe that they are indeed being productive. The truth is that the quality of the encoding from short-term to long-term memory is poor and filled with distractions and lack of quality revision time.

The remedy for the above:

- Moderate discipline
- A well-structured revision timetable
- The adoption of a positive mind set

Find your material. Getting access to the right material to study is central to success in revision. That is why it also preferable to have more than one source of information. It never ceases to amaze me that students often quibble about buying more than one text source for a subject. Students should always have access to at least three or four different sources and various online approved sources, including You Tube. Students should have access to:

- Up-to-date and correct specification
- Suggested recommended texts

- Additional texts: US texts are often useful for visual learning

- A dictionary – both English and subject-specific, e.g. economics

- Student work books – approved by their exam board

- Webography of useful resources

- Past papers

Organise yourself and your environment. The place and the way you learn is vital to your success. Everyone learns in their own way, but it is important to **reduce unnecessary distractions** that can prevent consolidation of learning and interfere with encoding of short-term into long-term memory. Try and reproduce the conditions in which you will be tested in order to learn and revise, i.e. a silent room, maybe a clock ticking away and a small, exam-type desk. This type of learning is called **state-dependent** and is learning associated with a particular state of mind.

Good ways to organise yourself and your environment:

- Have everything you need around for quick access – this makes learning efficient

- Ensure that you organise your notes in a logical order – have access to past papers and the specification

- Have access to examiners' reports and model answers from the exam boards

- Ensure that the room where you work is at a good temperature and that you have no major noise distractions

- Revise for 20-40 minutes, stop, take a break and do something quite mindless, like kicking a ball or something very basic and not demanding

- Make summary notes using key terms and create time limits on when things should be learnt by: in effect, give yourself a time-limited challenge

- Sometimes, it can help to revise and relax oneself with some very low classical music in the background

Bad ways to organise yourself and your environment:

- Revise with loud music in one's ears or in the background

- With a messy file and notes all over the room

- With no access to past papers, examiners' reports, the specification, textbooks, etc.

- Revise in a room that is too cold or too hot

- Spend too much time on one subject

- Revise for hours on end without a break

- Revise a topic and then engage in an activity that dilutes or **displaces** what has been learnt

Learning: Comprehension and Memory

Learning cannot really be achieved unless someone has understood the concepts involved. Before any student can progress, they must first grasp the basic principles of the topic – the necessary definitions, key words, phrases, people and concepts. Once this has been achieved, the process of learning, such that it can be recalled for examination purposes or direct application, has to be achieved.

Encoding, the process of creating a new memory, normally involves converting short-term memory (STM) into long-term memory (LTM). Most important memories for revision and learning are long-term. When revising, students encode by using their sensory and short-term memory, which get ultimately fixed in the long-term memory. In order to convert from STM into LTM, it is important that you are paying **attention.**

Once you have a long-term memory, you will have to access it. **REMEMBER, most information and knowledge in your head is available, just not accessible.** Accessing information, facts, data, etc. is ultimately down to your ability to access the memory under the stresses of exam conditions. How many times have students left an examination only to check a book or their notes and go "Damn – I knew that, I just could not remember it". This reinforces the importance of the quality of the encoding when revising and the need for **periodic repetition** in order to strengthen the synaptic (chemical) connections in the brain.

Your brain has an unlimited capacity to learn – it has over 100 trillion synapses. It is a sponge that can never become soaked with knowledge – your brain can never be full. It can get tired, but that is why it is so important when revising and learning to respect the following:

- Get a good night's sleep – a sleep-deprived brain cannot function efficiently

- Pay **attention** when learning – which means you must remove as many distractions as possible

- Achieve quality attention, hence encoding of LTM can only really be achieved in 20-30 minute intervals, followed by short breaks, then a return to study

- Do not skip breakfast – remember, compared with other organs, your brain is one of the highest consumers of glucose in your body – so feed it!

Revising with friends is only a good idea if you do not understand the topic. Once you have understood it and need to memorise it for recall, then revising with friends creates unnecessary distractions.

Ways to Improve Your Memory

Structure within your revision notes. If your notes have a logical, digestible structure, then they are more likely to be learnt: in other words, you create mini learning platforms for yourself.

Visual learning. We have very much evolved to learn visually – it is one of our memory's powerful capabilities, in particular face recognition. Using books that have coloured diagrams or having access to approved YouTube clips or other types of animated online learning can be a very effective way of understanding and memorising.

Memory techniques. Much is written about memory techniques, but many are somewhat overrated unless practised, in which case they can be very effective. What, however, is clear is that unlike your intellect or IQ, which cannot really be much improved upon using current techniques of measuring, **your memory, by contrast, can be significantly improved with**

practice and techniques. Some basic memory techniques include:

- Chunking

- Mnemonics

- The journey system

- The Roman room system

- Association

Let's look at each of these techniques:

CHUNKING

Given that our short-term memory seems to limit our ability to store more than seven or so items, chunking is a very simple, but effective method of remembering lists longer than this. It works by creating clusters of numbers or relating words together, making them easier to recall. For example, if you had to remember the number or code as follows – 392731938 – you could easily break it down and 'chunk' it to 39, 2731, 1938, which allows someone to more easily recall such a number.

MNEMONICS

A mnemonic is a type of memory aid that facilitates recall by making it easier for the user to access the information. Different types and mechanisms of mnemonics are recognised, such as:

Music/rhymes – e.g. children learn their alphabet by singing the ABC song or use the rhyme Thirty Days Hath September to remember the number of days in each month.

Names – e.g. to remember the colours of the rainbow use ROY G. BIV – red, orange, yellow, green, blue, indigo, violet.

THE JOURNEY SYSTEM

This is a highly effective form of specific mnemonic that helps people remember and recalls items by remembering specific landmarks on a journey. So, for example, if you walk to school or college, then you probably remember all the specific landmarks on that journey. If you had to recall ten key points for a history essay on the 'Principal reasons why the League of Nations failed', then you could more easily recall your ten key essay points or arguments by associating each one with a specific landmark on your journey to school. Central to this technique is the power of **visual memory**.

THE ROMAN ROOM SYSTEM

This very old technique involves the use of visual memory in a similar way to the journey system. With origins back to ancient Greece and Rome, the technique relies on recall of familiar objects within one's house or, more specifically, within a room. Sometimes called 'The Method of Loci' it requires the user to associate key ideas that need to be recalled with specific items. Most students have a very clear and detailed memory of their bedroom so could use this system to help facilitate recall.

ASSOCIATION

Association is at the heart of all memory techniques and in many ways is the common theme of the above techniques. Memory works through connecting to some other idea or term. For example, when one considers a specific large animal, such as a buffalo or elephant, we normally associate these animals with a particular trait or behaviour. By creating associations, our memories are enhanced. A child recalls an elephant because of its size and trunk, a lion by its roar or mane. Sometimes, associates work best when they are odd or funny. For example, if you had to remember your hotel name – the

Radisson, for example, you might associate it with a radish! Association techniques can be usefully applied at both GCSE and A-levels and students can make them as funny and bizarre as they like, so long as they work!

- *What is important to take with you about memory techniques is that you have to find your own system.*

Consolidation

Consolidation in learning refers to the stabilisation of memory trace after initial acquisition of the memory. Memory can decay over time unless consolidated through practice and repetition, which strengthen syntactic connections. Be warned, I am not suggesting that learning something over and over again equates to understanding – it does not. One must first comprehend, but then reasonable familiarity helps strengthen the memory and improves recall. Looking at something once is usually not enough - it usually requires at least five attempts, especially if it is a difficult concept. Multiple attempts are just self-defeating. So it is very important to keep practising topics and revisit them on a regular basis to reinforce the connections in the brain. It is very important to try and secure a whole understanding or gestalt of what you are learning. A gestalt is a way of looking for an essence or shape of an entity's complete form. It is very important for students to try and get a gestalt of a specific problem when trying to learn. It results from the interplay of language, information, logic, and the ability to connect things together to form a complete concept. For example, something as complex as evolution in biology requires a series of different concepts to fit together in order for the student to finally get the moment when it makes more sense.

CASE STUDY

In order to try and raise the profile of your school and its reputation, having a **centre for learning and revision** seems like a good idea. It makes perfect business sense to highlight a **key competence** – and what could be a better **reputational capability** than showing other students and their parents that your school has a capability in the area of revision and learning. What is important is to convey this key capability and 'sell it' to stakeholders in a way that demonstrates three important things. First, **credibility and competence** – having a centre for learning and revision at the school gives the school academic credibility, especially if it is overseen by those who have ability to deliver. Second, having an organised and dedicated centre to learning and revision provides the school with a **brand** that provides both functional and psychological benefits to students and their parents. Third, the centre also provides a platform to communicate a powerful **value proposition** – "Our school really cares about learning" – which also provides points of difference from the competition **(positioning)**.

All of the above can lead to growth and sustainability, which all brands and organisations strive to achieve and which are the essence of business strategy.

Chapter Summary

Effective learning is not that difficult, but rarely comes easily. You must recognise your bad habits and barriers to learning – remove or reduce them – and accept that you need some degree of discipline. You also need to create the right environment for learning and have access to the right resources. You cannot become a 'victim' of stereotypical thinking about your abilities as this only reinforces negative thinking and framing. One must, however, be realistic – you may not be a maths wizard, but that does not mean that you are simply 'no good at maths' – that's just plain defeatism. It is also dangerous thinking. All of us fail every now and then – that's perfectly normal. It's what you do with the failure and how you improve that counts. So never give up, never give in, be realistic, and enjoy the most wonderful thing in life – continuous learning and discovery.

Further Reading

How to Develop a Brilliant Memory, Dominic O'Brien (Duncan Baird Publishers)

Buzan's Study Skills, Tony Buzan (BBC Active)

Memory Improvement: How to Improve Your Memory in Just 30 Days, Ron White (BBC Active)

How to Pass Exams, Dominic O'Brien (Duncan Baird Publishers)

Final Word

The authors hope you have enjoyed reading this book and have found it useful in developing skills for the future. Do join us on Facebook and Twitter. We welcome your comments about the book and encourage you to share your thoughts and advice with other readers.

facebook.com/sixthformmba

twitter.com/SixthFormMBA

Finally we would like to leave you with a short anecdote, which is very relevant to the contents of this book. Many years ago, the famous golfer and sportsman – Gary Player – was being interviewed. During the interview the reporter said that he thought Gary had been lucky in his career. After a little reflection the golfer replied: "Yes, I guess I have been lucky. But the funny thing is, the more I practise, the luckier I get!"

Carpe Diem and good luck in your life and career!

www.thorogoodpublishing.co.uk